I'm most impressed with *Wealth i*  highly valuable information that anyone can apply to live a financially secure life. I recommend buying it today.

- Daniel Burrus, Leading Technology Forecaster,
Technotrends

Machtig has been on the leading edge of change in the financial services industry for over 10 years. Read his thoughts …listen to his words…he can make a difference in your financial and personal growth.

- Steve Barger, Senior Executive Vice President, Primerica

Your first reaction upon reading this book is "I can do this!" Your second reaction is "I wish I'd had this book sooner." No other book lays out such simple terms and intriguing methods to follow to create your own personal wealth.

- Robert Thele, President and CEO
Covey Leadership Center

I've read many books on what to do in the markets. Mr. Machtig has eclipsed all of them. He not only tells the reader what to do...but exactly how and when. He writes all of this in a simple, understandable style. This is the best personal finance book on the market. I wish this book was available ten years ago.

Richard Sapio, President and CEO
1-800-MUTUALS, Inc.

Wealth in a Decade sends a message to each of it's readers, that choosing to take control of your own financial choices and committing to a personal savings and investment program can prove to be a very profitable experience. This book is easy to read and comprehend. A must for serious investors.

Betty Sinnock, Co-Author — *The Beardstown Ladies
Common-Sense Investment Guide*

Wealth in a Decade is by far one of the best works on tangible wealth building available. A must read for growth oriented investors!

Thomas J. Winninger, CSP, CPAE
CEO Winninger Companies, Inc.
Past President of National Speakers Association

Finally, there is a personal investment book based on common sense and practical experience! In a world that has become increasingly precarious for the individual investor, Brett Machtig has summarized ten key investment principles that will guide all, who systematically follow them, toward financial security.

- Steve Merrell, Portfolio Manager,
American Express Financial Corporation

Brett doesn't waste time trying to impress us with how much he knows. He just cuts to the chase and gives us the answers we need to become financially independent in ten years. *Wealth in a Decade* provides us with a road map to financial independence that's easy to understand and put into practice.

- Robert A. Ortalda, Jr., CPA
*How to Live Within Your Means and
Still Finance Your Dreams*

Machtig walks his talk. He practices what he preaches to others. I have watched this book evolve as he interviewed over 100 people that are presently multi-millionaires. I know the financial mentors he has and how they have guided him along the way.

- Steve Anderson, President and CEO of CCC, Inc.

Wealth in a Decade

Wealth In A Decade

A fresh approach to financial freedom, security and control

WEALTH
I N A
DECADE

BRETT MACHTIG
with Ryan D. Behrends

Forward by Harry Dent

**Published by
Image Publishing
16997 New Market Drive
Eden Prairie, MN 55347
(800) 708-0558**

Cover Design
DX Electronic Production Studio

Editors
Audrey E. De La Martre
Linda J. Rening, Ph. D.

Wealth In A Decade™
ISBN 1-887494-01-4

Dedication

This book is dedicated to those investors who have learned the inherent laws of investing from the most expensive educational system there is, the School of Hard Knocks.

Brett Machtig

Acknowledgements

Sincere thanks to everyone who made this book possible:

To Steven W. Anderson who gave inspiration and structure to the Ten Laws around which this book is based.

To my wonderful clients whose changing investment requirements constantly challenge me to develop solutions to specific investment problems. A special thanks to those of you who lived the financial stories presented. You each have a special place in my heart.

To my firm, which has given me the freedom to examine the full range of investment products and to make meaningful and appropriate recommendations to meet the needs of clients, while offering opportunities for continued education, financial growth and personal development.

To the editors, publishers and project managers.

To my wife, Mary Carn-Machtig, for editing and material development, and especially for supporting the time taken from our evenings and weekends.

To Ryan Behrends, who has been involved with this project in one form or another for over 5 years. His research, writing, editing and the contribution of many additional thoughts and concepts have been an invaluable addition to this project.

To the many mentors who have contributed to this project: Daniel Burrus, Paul Zane Pilzer, John Naisbitt, Michael Basch, Mark Victor Hanson, Bob Thele, Ken Blanchard, Tim Pesut, Debra Jones, Tom Winninger, Dan Poynter.

To the many contributors to this book: Kristen Lund, Louis Navellier, Betty Sinnock of the Beardstown Ladies, and Lee Kopp.

And, finally, to God for giving all of us the energy, perseverance, and inspiration to complete this project.

WEALTH defined

You are wealthy when you are able to live from the return generated by your investment portfolio.

Wealth In A Decade

Table of Contents

Disclaimer

We live today in a highly litigious society and often like to sue each other, blame each other, and transfer responsibility to others.

Responsibility is a continuing theme of this book, and this space, traditionally used for what lawyers refer to as the "disclaimer", is also being used to make a more important point.

You've seen the words many times: "The investment principles, strategies and concepts presented in this book do not reflect the policies, or express the opinion, of any securities firm. Neither this book, nor any opinion expressed herein, should be construed as an offer to buy or sell any securities. Any strategies presented should not be implemented without first consulting a trusted investment advisor, attorney or accountant;" and "all client case histories are based on fact although elements may have been enhanced for the purpose of topical continuity or content evolvement. None of the persons depicted are real persons, nor are they meant to resemble anyone living or deceased, but are amalgams of the stories of many different people…" or words to that effect.

Today, disclaimers are a legal necessity, but they are a cop-out. The material in this book is no substitute for the reader taking personal responsibility for his or her own financial well-being and give no reason for thinking that the reader is featured in the text. If you need disclaimers, here they are. But I hope you will be more inclined to engage yourself in taking full charge of your own life.

What I have to say in the pages ahead offers you the opportunity to change your life and give you the financial security, control, and freedom you deserve.

Foreword

The Greatest Decade in History for Building Wealth

We are on the verge of the greatest boom in history. A period of high growth, high productivity and wage gains, low inflation, rising savings and falling debt ratios. *Wealth in a Decade* may be the most important book you read. For in it, Brett Machtig outlines a solid, conservative and proven way to build wealth for people of all income levels — in a decade — and that is about what we have to build security for our future while the economic winds continue to blow very strongly in our favor.

We are moving into the greatest economic surge in history not because of anything government or industry or individuals are planning to do, but because of fundamental trends already set in motion by the baby boom generation. And we can understand these trends because they are driven by everyday people like you and me. This boom will result from the powerful confluence of two very projectable trends: The largest generation born in history is going to move predictably into their peak years of earning and spending, while the most powerful technologies in history move out of niche markets into mainstream affordability and application.

New technologies, industries and work methods emerge into our economy every other generation, or about every 80 years. The last great economic revolution came to a crescendo in the Roaring 20s as the peak spending of the Henry Ford generation coincided with the emergence of cars, electricity, phones and many new products like Coca-Cola, into mainstream affordability driven by the powerful assembly-line revolution in work. It all came together in a decade of high growth, high productivity, low inflation, rising savings and falling debt ratios.

The size of this generation and the power of information technologies is much greater than the forces driving the Roaring 20s. I call this period ahead the "Roaring 2000s." In the introduction to Part II, Brett outlines the key points and charts from my first book, *The Great Boom Ahead,* and the summary insights from a great book by Daniel Burrus, *Technotrends.* It is time to stop listening to economists, politicians, and the media whine and fret over the obvious decline of our old economy, technologies, corporate structures, jobs, school systems, and so on. This is a unique period ahead. How and where we work and live will change more than any time in history. Therefore, we and all of society must change.

We simply have to understand that for a new era of prosperity with better jobs, a higher quality of life, and a higher standard of living to emerge, our old economy has to die. Do you realize that the assembly line revolution advanced the standard of living of the average worker in the U.S. nine times adjusted for inflation? Do you realize that the railroads, the telegraph companies, the coal companies, and many other companies that were the largest sectors of our economy, were decimated in the Roaring 20s? They just downsized forever. Do you realize that jobs changed dramatically from the Roaring 20s on, and that workers fought and resisted, at first, the very changes that advanced their standard of living so dramatically?

It's time to understand the most powerful forces in history and get with the new program. And these changes are in essence very simple and understandable. How our economy will evolve, how our companies will change, how our work and skills will advance is very clear and projectable. Why? The best companies, like Ford in the early 1900s have already proven the way, showing us where the growth markets are, how to use new technologies, and what the new work and organizational structures look like. And the new "smart" companies from Microsoft to Intel to Ben & Jerry's to Starbucks Coffee are not laying off workers. They are fun to work at and offer very bright career futures. I outline these changes in my second book, *Job Shock*.

But the most important foundation for preparing to enter the new era of prosperity comes in your personal life and finances. You need to have the financial flexibility to adapt to an economy where the typical person may have more like seven careers instead of one or two in a lifetime. Baby boomers will live longer than any generation and have less support from government programs like Social Security and Medi-Care because of the smaller generation that will be supporting them in retirement. More baby boomers and baby busters will want to start their own business. And baby boomers are coming out of a period where they had to pay the highest mortgage rates and housing prices in history, which forced them to incur higher debt loads than any generation in history.

The point is simple: We have to learn to save systematically and invest to secure our future. Brett Machtig shows us step-by-step how to do this in a way that is totally appropriate and achievable for families and individuals in any income range. Another important pay-off: The workplace of the future is going to demand people who can manage their own business or work in self-managing work teams. The best place to start to prepare is to run your own household like a business and become responsible for your own revenues, costs, and net worth.

This is not just a book for the wealthy, although they will benefit likewise from the proven wisdom in this book. If we follow what Brett is recommending and take the time to master his Ten Universal Laws of Creating Wealth, we will be greatly rewarded by the strength of the financial markets in the next decade plus. And we must start now. My rigorous study of family spending habits and their impact on the economy shows that the third and largest wave of baby boom spending will cause a dramatic surge in growth between late 1998 and 2007.

That is why this book is so timely. The next few years may be the last chance to buy stocks and mutual funds at reasonable prices before they accelerate into a Dow peak of 8,500 to 10,000 by 2007. The next decade will be the perfect time to build "wealth in a decade."

So please take the time to carefully consider the principles presented in this book. Then make the personal commitment to set in place the goals and systems by which you can guarantee your retirement, and even more important, your control over your own life and destiny. There may never be a better time for you to achieve what you want in life than in the coming decade. Best of success to you!

> \- Harry S. Dent, Jr.
> Author of *The Great Boom Ahead* and
> *Job Shock* and *H.S. Dent Forecast* newsletter
> MBA - Harvard Business School

Preface

Working with hundreds of brokers and investors who represent millions of dollars invested in the financial markets has shown me the same kinds of investment mistakes committed again and again. Novice investors, of course, prefer to become successful without making these mistakes or falling into the same traps. I agree, so I have analyzed the mistakes of others, coupled with an analysis of my own mistakes, summarized the fundamental lessons that successful investors have learned, and identified some of the traps that sometimes can catch even experienced investors. From that process evolved the principles that ultimately became the Ten Laws which are the foundation of this book.

Typically, inexperienced investors become experienced investors by making good and bad choices, finally learning over time to avoid the bad ones. Given the opportunity, I'm sure most investors would prefer to avoid those expensive lessons in the ever-changing world of investing. That's why I consider experienced as well as novice investors as my audience.

For a long time I've wanted to write a book for conservative investors who want their investments to earn dependably but not necessarily with great flair. At first I thought I'd put off writing this book until I was near retirement age, when I could use my status as an experienced, successful investor as an example for readers to follow to gain riches and security. However, as I lived, learned and invested, I soon realized that what works for one investor seldom works in exactly the same way for another. And, as time went by, my clients demonstrated the lesson taught by the fable about the tortoise and the hare: steady, lower risk investing coupled with understanding and living within your means ultimately lead to real wealth.

I've seen too many people work hard all their lives and reach the judgment day of retirement to discover that financially they can't afford to retire. What happened? Where did they go wrong? Were they victims of bad advice? Was their life so full of setbacks that they couldn't recover financially? Did they have bad luck? Did they spend their money on short term benefits and forfeit any hope for long term security?

There's no stock answer to those questions or, indeed, about investment procedures and products in general that would be applicable to every situation and investor. Investment opportunities abound. It is wise to ask yourself which are best for you at 20, 30, 40, 50, 60, even 70 years of age. Should you buy only no-load mutual funds? Will your money be safe in gold? When should you put your dollars into an annuity with the guarantee of lifetime income? Are AAA-rated municipal bonds the right place to be? Or are church bonds more secure? What about commodities like oranges, oil, and pork bellies, or limited partnerships in land and buildings? What about unit investment trusts, collectibles, foreign stocks, closed-end mutual funds, futures or real estate? Will you be paid the promised high returns? Yes, the number of investment choices today seem nearly unlimited.

If you've got a buck, it seems someone has an ideal investment product. In a typical sales presentation you'll hear wonderful reasons why a particular investment is perfect for your needs. Which investment product is discussed doesn't seem to matter; it only changes the seller's focus. For example, you might be told, "Widely diversified products are safest because, if one stock goes down, your portfolio of investments won't be greatly affected." Conversely you could hear, "Narrowly focused portfolios are best because, if one stock goes up, you can realize a larger profit."

Interest rates affect returns, so an advisor might say: "Long term products assure safety because interest rates are more likely to go down than up." Then, there are short-term investments that allow you to cash out more quickly so you can take advantage of a rising interest rate market.

Are you considering commission cost? No-load products appear to save you from paying sales commissions. No-fee products save money because the sales fee is paid by the issuer.

Worried about safety? Some products are backed by a government, guaranteed by the integrity of the issuer, or insured by some agency or organization. They can be AAA-rated, investment grade, or high yield. The list of claimed advantages and benefits of investment ownership goes on and on.

Invariably, problems don't seem to occur until after your check has cleared your bank. Once you own a particular investment, things start to happen that weren't mentioned. You notice that your safe, secure, can't-miss investment has decreased in value. "Well," they explain, "the 10% guaranteed internal rate of return is really only 4.98% compounded annually." Or, "Oh, it's guaranteed from default, but that doesn't mean it won't go down in value before it matures."

Some investors have been surprised to hear, "Yes, it's insured. What that means is that your principal can't be lost, but interest payments may not be made." Other standard answers to disappointed investors are:

"Of course it is government backed, by the government of Oz."

"This really isn't a fee, its just the usual processing and handling charge."

"No-load doesn't mean no costs."

"Your investment is secure, and now that the price has gone down, it's time to buy some more. We call it dollar cost averaging."

Into what stone is it carved that you always have to learn from experience, especially bad experience? Wouldn't it be great to get the whole story before you make an investment? Wouldn't you prefer to hear the potential for downside risk, expressed in accurate, easy-to-understand language, before you put your cash into an investment?

Clients encouraged me to write this book now, not later at retirement age, because they wanted that kind of information. They asked me to cut through the confusion of new investment opportunities to give more people the chance to be better informed, to show how to ask meaningful questions, and to become more comfortable with the principles of successful long-term investing.

In response to their urgings I have written this book for you, the average investor who has accumulated a nest egg, or for you, the investor who recognizes the need to establish a meaningful financial plan to protect your future. I want to help you build personal prosperity to allow you to live a full life of peace and contentment when you decide to retire. I also want to present the information in incremental steps that will bring you small successes on the way to achieving your overall goals.

This is a book for beginning and serious investors that lays out the wealth-building process and the road that gets you to financial success. Even if you are following 90% of the laws presented here, the 10% you aren't following could cost you your security. My aim is to help you achieve financial security.

By law, I can't make specific recommendations, but I can and do give examples based on those specific investor circumstances that appear in the case histories. Please note, however, that they are presented as a teaching guide, not as an absolute investment rule.

Over time, investment theories are tested by war, political change, tax law reforms, and new economic policy. Those that have passed these tests will be discussed in detail here so you can understand how they can work for you. The bottom line is that your portfolio must meet your needs, which will change as economic, political and personal conditions change. You must be alert to these changes and be ready to meet them. To help you do this, I provide information so you can make choices more easily and profitably.

Even after you learn how to use this book and how to be a prudent investor, you can still have investment setbacks. Indeed, professional investors who have observed the markets for many years can be surprised by financial events. Nonetheless, it's my goal to teach you enough to lessen the severity of normal investment setbacks. The only sure way to avoid investment failure entirely is not to invest. On the other hand, one investment failure in a carefully planned and managed portfolio doesn't mean that the whole portfolio is vulnerable to financial ruin.

One final note: The information and strategies presented in this book have been compiled from over ten years of working with investors, researching and learning from the markets. These laws have not always been there to follow, so I, too, have made mistakes from which I've learned. The financial markets can teach a different lesson every day and will still be instructing investors long after I am gone. But, I believe that you can capitalize on the mistakes I have made and the lessons I have learned.

If you have any questions, please refer to the back of the book for information on how to reach me personally. I welcome your questions, comments, and concerns.

-Brett Machtig

Wealth In A Decade

PART ONE

The Ten Universal Laws of Creating Wealth

Wealth In A Decade

Introduction to Part I

Welcome to the wonderful world of intelligent investors! You have earned your opportunity to invest by spending less money than you earn. The concepts presented in this book can be used by investors of all ages, all income levels, all socio-economic groups, and all portfolio sizes, to dramatically increase their capital base. Self-discipline is the most important quality you need to be successful at building an investment portfolio. By applying the principles and the lessons learned from the cases presented here, you can become and remain wealthy. In addition, you will experience freedom, security, and control in your life.

The American Heritage Dictionary defines wealth as "a great quantity of valuable material possessions or resources." I don't aspire to a goal so grand, general or vague. In my vocabulary, wealthy people are those who can live off their investments. They have reached the point where their capital available for investments is working for them in a portfolio that supports them financially without any added time or effort on their part.

I accept that setting money aside today is difficult. Demands for cash come from every direction. It's more fun, and much easier, to spend than to save. But some people do save and have fun. You can, too.

First, let's explore some questions that potential investors ask. Who is wealthy? How can I become wealthy? How can I tell if I am on track to becoming wealthy? Will I feel different when I am wealthy? How can I stay wealthy?

Who Are The Wealthy? You and I know people who appear to be rich. They live in expensive houses, belong to country clubs, travel the world, dress in the latest fashions, have expensive new cars and boats, and have high-paying jobs. The truth in many cases is that they live from paycheck to paycheck, albeit a big pay-check. They are the mock rich. My experience reveals an inverse relationship between the amount of ostentatious wealth and the size of an investment portfolio. That's because the more money people spend on possessions, the less money they have available for investment. Yes, there are exceptions, but the sad fact is that most of the people who appear to be rich, aren't financially secure. However, I believe anyone who has a plan, self-discipline, investment knowledge and a bit of patience can be wealthy.

Most of the wealthy people I represent have retired. Most earned a good living. Some had incredibly good luck. But earning a good wage, salary or commission, or getting lucky once couldn't have guaranteed their financial independence if they had spent more than they earned. In fact, the people whose lifestyles match their high incomes find that they need to amass larger portfolios to continue to generate that high income after retirement. This can create a conflict of priorities which gets in the way of building adequate wealth during their income-earning years.

By contrast, I have clients who have never earned much money, didn't inherit a cent, and wouldn't know how to buy a new car, a vacation spa, or an array of precious gems. As one client remarked, "I have always been told that I worked for peanuts. Well maybe I did, but I saved as many of those peanuts as I could. Then when the time came, I made peanut butter out of them."

Her peanut-butter portfolio currently is valued at $500,000. It earns income of nearly $50,000 per year. Add her social security income, subtract her expenses, and she's genuinely wealthy. She lives comfortably on the income generated by her investments, which is quite a remarkable payoff for someone whose annual wages were never more than $25,000.

My average client is somewhere between 50 and 70 years old. When they came to me for advice at 40, 50, or 60, I asked them, "What took so long? Why are you just now beginning to worry about your financial security? What would you have done differently knowing what you know today?"

Their responses echoed the same history: It took time to accumulate the toys they wanted and then develop the self-discipline necessary to save. Having children, satisfying their need for toys, and providing everyday living expenses soaked up their cash flow. Every increase in income was absorbed immediately into the cash outflow. Family necessities grew with the children's changing needs, including college tuition and weddings. Even after the children left the nest, their expenses were still the parents' biggest unexpected financial drains.

These clients consistently indicated that they had no life plan. That meant they lived and learned by the seat of their pants, constantly being surprised by unexpected expenses. As a result, they lived most of their adult lives in debt, unable to build significant savings until their debts were paid. But once retirement loomed, they panicked and got serious about saving. And once they started to make saving a high priority, most built the savings they had in less than ten years.

They also told me the importance of working together with their spouse in the financial planning process so unified goals could be set and met. More often than not, one spouse will be left alone because of the death of the other. The surviving spouse will have to get along on the income generated by the investment portfolio they both created during marriage.

What about inheritance? The old cliché, "Grandpa earned it, dad used it and the kids spent it," is no longer true. Today, most parents have it spent long before the kids have a chance. Wealth is rarely inherited. Most often it's earned and saved the old fashioned way, through hard work and careful spending patterns. There are exceptions, but they are just that, exceptions. The all-important rule to building wealth is to spend less than you receive.

Who is wealthy? Those who have established a portfolio that will provide security and comfort. The actual dollar amount will vary depending on the person or couple. Some will need more, others less. As I said earlier, portfolio size and content combined with expected financial needs is the critical factor in determining financial goals.

Consider this question: How much do I need to save today to meet my financial needs tomorrow? This book will help you develop the answer that's right for today and will help you prepare for tomorrow.

How Can You Become Wealthy? First comes desire; you must want wealth enough to keep your spending habits under control. Control is hard to maintain as merchants get better at convincing us that material goods and pleasures are necessities. The problem is that spending to gratify today's wishes prevents you from building a portfolio to purchase tomorrow's necessities or pleasures. The key is to strike a balance between instant gratification and planning for long-term security, freedom, and financial control.

If you're satisfied with all current aspects of your investment portfolio, you can skip the next few paragraphs. If you haven't started your portfolio or feel that it's inadequate, read on through some truisms of investment strategy.

Except for your home, never, never go into debt. If you're in debt now, pay it off before buying any more non-essential items. In chapter two is a step-by-step process on how to be debt-free. Even a car, a college education, or a vacation is something you can anticipate and include in your budget.

While a car is the second most expensive purchase you'll ever make, it isn't an investment, unless it's a collectible with an inherent value to other collectors. Most cars merely lose value and require maintenance. A car may be a necessity, but no one needs to buy a new one every two or three years.

I learned that lesson with simple arithmetic when I was 23 years old. I paid out $19,900 on a 60-month easy payment plan of $452 per month. After paying on the loan for about three years, I paid it off by selling the car for the outstanding loan value. My net cost to own that car was $15,820, or $5,273 per year. The point is that if you must buy a car, pay cash, and buy cars that are at least one year old, if not two or three years old. Had I done that, I would have been able to invest the difference, perhaps as much as $10,000, and been none the worse for transportation. In five years, at 10% interest, the $10,000 would have grown to over $16,000, and by my retirement, this $10,000 would have equaled over $550,000 in my portfolio.

Another lesson I learned was to pay off every credit charge within the period of free use of the money. My wife, Mary, and I keep our cash invested, earning interest until we have to withdraw it to pay bills. Until you can pay for your living expenses out of your current income, you can't begin a serious investment portfolio.

How Will You Know if You Are on Track To Becoming Wealthy? The answer is different for everyone, but there are some broad guidelines you can follow to chart your progress. If you're below age 20, probably you have a part-time job, perhaps an allowance, and cash gifts from relatives available for spending. How much do you spend on investments? If the answer is "none" you're on the wrong track. Unfortunately, the wrong track is standard for most youth.

One of my clients told me that it seemed he had been trained from birth to invest any spare cash. His investment account was started for him by his parents out of christening gifts. They obtained a social security number for him when he was seven days old and a Uniform Gifts to Minors (UGMA) account was opened when he was ten days old. By the time he was ready for college, he was able to self-fund his education.

As luck would have it, he qualified for a scholarship that reduced the need to use his savings. In his sophomore year he moved out on his own and he was totally self sufficient before he was 20, with a serviceable car and over $20,000 in savings. He was on track to becoming wealthy. He had developed thrift habits that would continue to serve him well.

If you don't have parental support, you can still save something on your own from part-time jobs. Five bucks a week for years does become $1,000, which is enough to begin an investment portfolio. Unfortunately, few children save, or if they do save they're not encouraged to invest their savings in their future.

By 30 you may have some opportunities to measure your progress in concrete terms. How did you fill in the personal financial statement your banker gave you when you came in to apply for your home loan? Did your assets consist only of clothing, furniture, fixtures and your car? Was your checking/savings balance below $5,000? Were you lucky enough to work for an employer who had an employee retirement fund, and your current vested value was about $10,000?

Or do you have big loans outstanding on two cars, a boat, a lake place and camper? Is your combined account balance with VISA, American Express, Master Card, and local department stores greater than 25% of your annual income?

Either way, you've got a problem. You're on the road to somewhere, but it is certainly not to wealth and financial independence.

On the other hand, I have a 30-year old client who has spent the last 10 years determining, then perfecting, a career path. She has a job in the industry she believes has a long future. She's married and has one child. She's paid off her outstanding college loans, her car is paid for, and she lives in a $125,000 home with a mortgage payment less than 25% of her net income. She has no other debt. Her financial accounts consist of a money market savings account that is accumulating funds for home improvements, and two Certificates of Deposit (CDs) valued at $10,000. In addition she has an IRA fund with a balance of nearly $25,000. She is on the road to wealth and already has a net worth of over $100,000.

By age 40, many people find themselves finally getting their financial affairs into order and may be approaching the break-even point. They have paid for their cars and are out of debt except for mortgage payments. These people often begin to experience career disillusionment because things aren't working out financially as they would like. Their children are still pretty young, but the threat of college expenses is on the horizon. If they're lucky and have been able to stay with the same employer long enough to get covered by a retirement program, their retirement fund has now grown to

$50,000. Similarly, if they have been fortunate enough to stay with the same spouse, their available checking/savings balance is about $10,000. Although they have begun to make improvements on their home by adding a deck and finishing the basement, they still haven't been able to begin their investment portfolio.

On the other hand, the purposeful investor has nearly paid off his $150,000 home and has $15,000 in cash. Funds for anticipated expenditures account for another $15,000, and a retirement account with his employer is worth about $110,000. And perhaps best of all, his investment portfolio is valued at nearly $150,000, giving him a visible net worth over $400,000 dollars. By some people's standards, he's already wealthy.

By 50, committed investors have reached the point where they're comfortable creating plans for retirement. Their investment portfolio has a value that can easily support the level of expenditure they're accustomed to. Their house has an appraised value of $200,000 with no mortgage. The operating cash accounts have a balance of about $30,000 and their investment portfolio is worth nearly $450,000. In addition, their retirement account balance is in the neighborhood of $330,000. Somewhere in the past few years they have created revocable trusts which allow them to shelter from taxes about $1.2 million, given 1995 tax law. They continue to control their spending habits and live within their means.

Contrast this to what happens to far too many others. At 50, they suddenly realize they don't have too many more years to work, so they try to cut back on spending and increase savings. Investment planners are hastily sought and then scurry about trying to find an investment with a sure-fire, high potential payoff to obtain a big multiplier factor for their investment. Thus they accept a huge risk they don't understand, until after they have lost their money.

The nightmare continues when they find out that their employer has invested their retirement funds in guaranteed insurance contracts (GICs) with an insurance company that has just filed for Chapter 11 bankruptcy, and their account is worth only a fraction of what it should have been. Their cash balance is about one month's pay, employment prospects are getting worse, and there is a second mortgage on the house to cover the lake place or college tuition for the kids. They do have an investment portfolio, but it is only about $100,000.

If these folks don't change something pretty soon, later in life they will find they must survive exclusively on a limited portfolio supplemented by the dole of Social Security. Social Security will contribute about $8-10,000 per year, and the $100,000 investment portfolio will contribute $10-12,000. If they're lucky, they can plan their retirement on an annual income of $18-22,000 before taxes. "No problem," you say if they can live on that. Unfortunately, many people can't. As a result, they must survive on an income lower than subsistence wages.

In the meantime, disciplined investors are looking at properties in Texas, Florida or Arizona for the winter months and deciding whether or not to move up north for the summer. They have $100-300,000 in assets available to supplement their portfolio earnings. Annual income is assured from their personal portfolio. Anything received from social security or an employer pension plan is extra and they certainly don't have to look for work.

At 70, some folks are so afraid of sudden death they won't buy green bananas. The reality is, some of these people may live for another 20 years or more. They mistakenly invest for the short term and, as a result, achieve inadequate rates of return when they most need the income. These people may have developed health problems, and perhaps a spouse has passed away. The nursing home looms, if they can find one that takes Medicare patients. In a word, their situation is grim. They're out of money. They can't live off portfolio income, because there isn't any. Their only income is about $1,000 a month from Social Security. At some point, these poor people are going to lose hope and live out their years in bitterness and regret.

Prudent investors may have problems, but need for money isn't one of them. Typically, by age 70, they have portfolios valued at $2-4 million. They have an ad hoc advisory board made up of an accountant, lawyer, and financial advisor, all of whom are consulted on a regular basis. As a result, these 70-year-old investors have set up portfolios to include provisions for estate planning. They are fully protected from inheritance taxes, probate, and the other expensive processing costs that occur after death. Their children have been trained on portfolio maintenance, or they are denied access. The portfolios are designed to be managed after their death, without interfering with the lives of the kids.

What does this all mean? It means that prudent investors have learned to live within their means. Their portfolio grows at a faster rate than expected and they don't feel compelled to spend the excess. Their conservative approach to living prevents them from spending money foolishly. Retirement for them becomes a blend of community service, travel and other activities that help them to stay healthy and live longer.

How Will You Know When You Become Wealthy? You are wealthy when you can live off your investments. This can occur when you are 21, 35, 47, or 54. Age isn't important. What is important is learning when to say no to uncontrolled spending.

There are other descriptions of being wealthy. You are wealthy when you have reached the point where your decision to go to work is not determined by financial need. You are wealthy if you can make a career change without regard to salary. You are wealthy if you can take time off from work to investigate a project that is important to you for non-financial reasons. And, you are wealthy when you volunteer your time to public charities without considering the financial ramifications to your income stream.

Ultimately, however, the only definition of wealth that matters is your own. Some people are quite content earning enough to provide them with their current standard of living. Others dream of sailing the world, having a private jet, or a second home. Whatever your personal goals, make sure the steps to those goals are small enough to climb, and follow the outline presented in this book to set your plan in motion.

How Can You Stay Wealthy? By saving money and making as few mistakes in your portfolio composition as possible, you will retain wealth. That is what this book is about. In Part One, I explain each of the ten universal laws of Creating Wealth. These laws are inescapable, much like the physical law of gravity. This book includes pointers on how to save, how to invest those savings during the years you have available to build a portfolio, and I try to demystify and make workable the whole process.

Don't despair if you were once wealthy but have wandered off the path. My research indicates that there have been many people who have achieved and lost wealth more than once. Divorce, business failure, extended disability or simply attempting to live TV's depiction of the affluent life are examples of things that have temporarily sidetracked some individuals. If you have wandered off the path, this book can get you started in the right direction again.

If you currently have a sizable portfolio, this book will help you to keep what you have. A great deal of time will be spent trying to get you to discover your actual risk tolerances. Many investors who have jumped on the mutual fund bandwagon in the last several years have never been through a protracted period of declining prices in the stock market. Because of this fact, most investors haven't stopped to ask themselves, "How much could I actually lose in the market?" Between January 1972 and June 1993, the worst case scenario for the S&P 500 from a high point to a low point was a drop of 43%.[1] I don't know how many investors who label themselves as aggressive would be able to tolerate a loss of that magnitude, stay in the market, or actually add money to the market.

In Part Two is a detailed description of each of the investment paths you can take to achieve your financial goals. In it, I will show you ways to create a portfolio that will generate the highest possible returns based on the risks you can accept. I didn't get the overall asset allocation strategy presented in Part Two from my college education, nor did I get it from the broker training program I went through. I didn't even get it from the vast amount of preparation it took to take the exams that allow me to be called a portfolio manager.

I came upon this strategy after interviewing over 100 people who had started with nothing and had accumulated multi-million dollar portfolios. There was a common theme running through the way they had their portfolios positioned, and I am going to share it with you.

Together we'll examine only those classes of assets that you need to use to become wealthy. I'll help you learn how, why and when to change a portfolio to capture the benefits possible from changing market conditions. I'll spend time explaining how to manage a portfolio to be sure that it is responsive to your changing needs. And, I'll cover what to do if you feel that you need help managing your investment. Finally, I'll suggest ways to teach your children and grandchildren all of the values you've learned.

This book is your important first investment. With it, you don't have to live as an indentured servant. Rather you will be more able to strive toward the goals of the U.S. Constitution: life, liberty, and the pursuit of happiness. Your payoff from following these strategies, principles, rules of thumb, and advice will probably be the highest payoff of any you receive as you build a lifestyle of consistent investing.

Footnotes

1 Myth vs. Reality, Campbell & Company, 1993 (brochure)

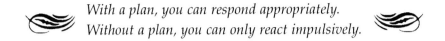

With a plan, you can respond appropriately.
Without a plan, you can only react impulsively.

Chapter One
The Law of Setting Goals

Enthusiasm for a new venture is stimulating, but setting goals is the first step of any successful venture. At least, that's been my experience. At age 16 I began setting goals for myself, and my experience has demonstrated that it's one of the most important things I have ever done. In fact, I'm so convinced of its importance that goal-setting rose quite naturally to the rank of the First Law of Creating Wealth.

When I was 16, my father introduced me to the business world through his film business. While other kids were out playing ball on the weekends, I was at conventions and attending meetings with my dad. By words and action, he gave me a work ethic and taught me the basics of the business world, even the important skill of making conversation during business dinners.

One evening we went out to dinner with a potential client. Although the man was quite young, I was surprised and impressed with how much he had accomplished. Over dinner I grilled him, much to my fathers dismay, about how he had become so successful so quickly. "Goals," he said.

He had taken a course by Jose Silva[1] that had changed his life because it started him on the path to regular and focused goal-setting. Immediately I sought out the course, only to discover that it cost $500. To me at 16, $500 might just as well have been a million dollars.

After thinking about it, I decided that if I was ever going to emulate this man's success, I would have to do some serious goal-setting. My first goal would be to do whatever it took to earn the $500 before The Silva Method's next seminar. After several month's work and saving, I had raised the fee and registered.

At the seminar I was overwhelmed by the range and amount of material covered. Throughout the seminar we were put through a series of goal-setting exercises. I had a grand total of four goals that were pretty typical of a 16-year-old, but certainly nothing to be ashamed of. The first goal was to become a straight A student, which was a stretch because at the time I was sporting a C average. This was an important goal because I intended to go on to college and would need better grades to be accepted. I was on the wrestling team in high school, so my second goal was that I would make it to the state tournament. My third goal was to replace my rusty Volkswagen, one that my grandfather gave me, with one of the fastest cars available. The final goal, and remember I was only 16, was to meet a nice girl.

Within six months, I had achieved every one of those goals: my grades were up to A, I wrestled in the state tournament, I replaced my VW with a Maserati Gibli SS, and I was dating a really special girl. Hey! This is pretty neat, I thought, and set more goals, each time setting my sights a little higher.

Setting a goal is not the same as achieving a goal. I worked very hard to achieve those first goals, and subsequent ones, and I learned that goals don't always work out. For example, when I was an undergraduate at MacMurray College, I set a goal to get a graduate degree from Duke University. While at

MacMurray, I met, fell in love with, and married a young woman from a small town in Illinois. We lived on love, because that's all there was. Things went well, other than being broke.

I got a full scholarship to Duke University's Fuqua School of Business in the form of a one-time lump sum payment for the first year. After I got the scholarship and began work at Duke, my wife succumbed to the culture shock of moving from a rural area to a bigger city, and we were divorced. In shock and broke again after the divorce settlement, I watched my two goals swirl down the same drain.

The lesson I learned was that goals need to be flexible enough to allow room for setbacks. Some goals will never be achieved. Sometimes it hurts, is upsetting, and feels like major failure. But failure allows a step back to gain new perspective and then to move forward again. That's the time to remember that there are no failures, only results.

Enjoy Your Achievements   One day when I was in my 20s, I was doing some computer work and I had the opportunity to meet with an executive in the computer industry. From our meeting, I learned another lesson about goal-setting.

One of the things that I found fascinating about visiting top executives was observing their offices. I liked to look around the office to see how it was decorated and what they had on their office walls. I figured that observing these features would give me a feel for what kind of a person I was dealing with. I noticed that his office was decorated sparingly. There were no awards or accolades on his walls. Instead, there were a few family pictures, a little art, and one wall featured a framed, gold embossed article from the Boston Globe dating back to the turn of the century.

The article was about a pastor who visited most of his congregation by train. In his travels he observed that people were always in a great hurry to get aboard the train. While they waited they damned the minutes. Once aboard the train they damned the minutes until they could get on the next train. I asked this executive why he had that particular article on his wall. He said he knew many people who lived their entire lives that way. Can't wait to get out of high school. Can't wait to get out of college. Can't wait to get married. Can't wait to buy a home. Can't wait to start a family. Can't wait until the kids are in school. Soon it's can't wait until retirement. Life, according to these rushing people, always will be perfect, but never is. And even if it were perfect at the plateau of each goal, these people wouldn't notice it, they'd never enjoy the gift of the goal achieved because they're too obsessed with the future. Each time he sat down to write out company goals, my host told me, he used the story for focus. He always allowed time to enjoy the fulfillment of one goal before moving on to the next.

That lesson is one of the pivotal things I've learned about goal-setting and, indeed, about living. If we enjoy the process of setting each goal and achieving it, we allow ourselves to enjoy each step along the way, and finally to enjoy our whole lives. Life is process, so if we enjoy only the completion of the goal and not the journey to it, we leave out most of life.[2]

Either They're Your Goals Or They're Not   You can choose to control your own destiny by setting your own goals, or you can choose to assume your destiny by default, submitting to chance or another's authority by failing to set goals. Either way you control yourself by deciding or failing to decide. Indeed, you can control nothing but yourself and your actions. So, either you accept responsibility for your own destiny or excuses can creep in and you will fall short of achieving your goals. You've heard lots of these excuses:

- I can't lose weight because I have to go to those business lunches with my boss.
- I didn't get the garage cleaned because the chatty neighbor came over.
- I couldn't save any money last year because my taxes are so high.

People who offer excuses like that are neither controlling themselves, nor accepting responsibility for controlling their own destinies and, worse, they put the blame for their failures on outside factors. Goals must embrace things you directly control, otherwise positive change won't happen. For example, if you're in sales and your goal is to be the top salesperson in your company, and you go after business with great enthusiasm and planning, you'll more than likely succeed. However, if your strategy is to wait for the customer to beat a path to your door with orders in hand, you won't succeed.

Find A Mentor A strategy that has really helped me with my goal-setting is finding people who are willing to be mentors and to share their wisdom with me. I have consciously sought and developed relationships with several people who live their lives, play their game, or run their business better than anyone else and are willing to share their knowledge. As their protégé I have learned valuable lessons without expensive trial-and-error experiences. There are many wheels I don't have to reinvent. If you and I are willing to follow the recipe of a master chef, we don't have to spend the 30 years she did to perfect a soufflé. Instead, we can turn our energies to perfecting a white sauce and one day teach it to protégés of our own.

My first experience with having a mentor began one summer day when I was 18. I was driving my Maserati Gibli through a residential neighborhood and spotted a gorgeous, forest green Jaguar 12 cylinder XKE convertible in a driveway. I stopped to get a closer look and began a conversation with the owner. As it happened, he was as interested in my car as I was in his, and we began to talk cars.

The conversation moved past cars and into other areas. I became fascinated with the stories he told about his work. He told me that he was the pilot for the Chairman of the Board and the officers of Motorola Corporation. With the help of a recommendation from this man, I got a job at Motorola as steward and janitor for the corporate air fleet. My job was to keep the hangar, planes and cars of the President, Vice Presidents and Chairman serviced and clean.

There I was, an 18-year-old kid, looking into a hangar with four aircraft used by four top corporate officers. I noticed that, while all the airplanes were nice, the one used by the Chairman of the Board was the best. Walking into the passenger compartment was like walking into an elegant and very expensive home: luxurious carpeting everywhere, expensive paintings on the walls, fine furnishings. I stared, more impressed than I had been with anything I had seen.

One day the Chairman of the Board was boarding his jet. He was in a particularly good mood that day and struck up a conversation with me. After a couple of minutes he asked me what I wanted to do when I finished college. I told him that I wanted his job, because it was the most interesting job I could think of. Of course, I had no idea exactly what he did. It seemed like the only thing he did was fly around in his jet.

He smiled, not unkindly. I went on to ask him exactly what skills and college course work I'd need to be able to do his job. Obligingly, he briefly outlined the skills that he thought were necessary. Although I didn't become the chairman of a Fortune 500 company, I followed his advice to the letter and it changed my life.

Kristin   Kristin is Vice President of an educational company that owns schools and educates families nationwide. In addition to supervising day to day operations, managing the company's 75 employees and marketing the company's products and services, Kristin is active in her community and enjoys quality time with family and friends. How does one accomplish this by the age of 24? Kristin is a master at mentoring.

Sometime during her college career, her father suggested that she learn from people who were the best at what they do by creating a personal Board of Directors. She first made a list of people whom she wanted her life to model. This list grows continually as she meets new people.

Her first mentor was Cathy, a vice president of a major database marketing company. Among the many things that Cathy taught Kristin was the fact that anyone you want to know is only three people away. Inspired by Cathy's undaunting enthusiasm and lust for life, Kristin realized that she had only to ask.

She approaches new interviewees with a letter explaining her admiration for their accomplishments and the way that they have chosen to live life. She briefly explains her passion for learning from the best and then requests a two hour interview in order to learn how they have become a master. "Before the interview, I do some digging to find out as much as I can about the person. Then I create a list of questions that is neither redundant nor boring. My objective is to know as much as possible about the interview so that our encounter may uncover tactics that even she may not have realized before."

Another of Kristin's mentor's is Sir John Templeton, the "Dean of Global Investing". During a visit to China with the World President Organization, she acted on a life long desire to meet this gentle, warm and gracious man. Not only did he accept the two hour interview, they have since become friends, and Kristin turns to him for advice on her life changing decisions.

According to Kristin, the goal with mentoring isn't necessarily finding high-profile people. The only pre-requisite is that the potential mentor has mastered something that you want to learn. "The mentors in my life have taught me many of my most valuable lessons and they have shown me how to create a better quality of life in all I do. Most importantly, my mentors have become my friends. God has blessed my life in so many ways, and I am eternally grateful for the gifts that these people continue to bring to my life."

Financial Goal-Setting   Why all this discussion about the inner workings of setting goals? Because I believe that insight into the process makes application of the process easier. Let's apply this general knowledge to setting financial goals. Remember, the process of setting financial goals is the very foundation of the whole concept of building wealth.

Unfortunately, I've found that setting financial goals is something most investors don't know they need to do, don't know how to do, or don't take the time to do. They begin their adult life with high hopes of financial success and security, but without specific goals to save money, the demands and temptations of living creep in, and savings procrastination takes over. The years slip by and soon a woefully underfunded retirement is at hand.

Two population dynamics are converging that will make the retirement years of many people a burden rather than the comfortable, secure time they envision. First, the largest percentage of the baby boom generation will retire at about the same time. Second, the human life span is increasing. Accordingly, boomer retirees will live longer, spreading out social security resources over more people and more years. Most experts agree that these two factors will combine to force critical changes on the social security system.

Unless major legislation is passed adding huge sums of money to social security, perhaps at the expense of other government programs or the national debt, one of two things will probably happen:

- Elimination of social security
- Slashing benefits to a fraction of the current payout

Neither option is particularly appealing for someone facing retirement in the next few decades. While this all may seem like a scare tactic trumped up by the financial services industry to help build its revenues, it isn't. The bare fact is that unless all average citizens of this country take responsibility for their retirement, they have every reason to be scared.

Identifiable Benefits of Goals   Yale University did a study that identified the benefits of goal setting. In 1954, the graduating class at Yale University was polled and each student was asked: Do you have specific, written financial goals? About 3% did. Twenty years later the same class was asked the same question again and the results revealed that the same 3% who had specific, written financial goals in 1954, had acquired more assets than the other 97% combined.[3]

Financial goal-setting may feel like an intimidating task, but it doesn't have to be. As a matter of fact, you may have a savings account, or a life insurance policy, or a will, all of which represent legitimate financial goals. Perhaps your savings account was set up to provide an emergency fund. Your life insurance policy is designed to provide for your loved ones in case something happens to you. Your will makes sure that your assets pass on to the people you choose.

Each of those strategies can be written into the future tense as though it's a financial goal:

- Set up an emergency fund
- Provide for family's financial security
- Ensure that assets are distributed at death

As you can see, when you look at it like this, setting financial goals does not seem as difficult.

The next step is to set some targets and give the goals a time frame, which allows you to set a monthly saving goal if need be. For example, if you want to buy a car in two years and would like to put down $3,000, you would need to save $125 a month. ($3,000/24 mos.)

Adding a time frame, the above goals could be restated as:

- Set up an emergency fund with three months income before the first of the year.
- Buy life insurance policy and pay premiums annually to provide for my family's security.
- Have will drafted immediately to ensure that my assets are distributed at death.

Not all financial goals are great, grand plans that will make you wealthy. Some are small, but they are no less important. For example, in your 20s a financial goal may be something as simple as establishing credit or opening savings accounts. Other goals for this age should be purchasing life and auto insurance, beginning to save in an IRA or other tax deferred investment plan and, once you have accumulated some assets, drafting a will.

As you enter your 30s, you may want to include the goals of establishing a college fund for your children, purchasing a home, implementing tax saving strategies, and an investment plan for your discretionary income.

As you begin your 40s, you may develop financial goals for purchasing a vacation home or cabin. You may need to revise your will or invest in municipal bonds, depending on your tax bracket.

Between age 50 and retirement your financial goals may include reallocating your investments gradually to a more conservative income bias. Perhaps you should include purchasing a long term care insurance policy or setting up an estate plan.

Finally, at retirement you will be able to reward yourself for a lifetime of diligent financial goal-setting. But wait, financial goal-setting shouldn't stop at retirement. At that time, financial goals may include fine-tuning your investment strategy for changing market conditions, establishing a living trust, giving to charity, giving gifts to your children to reduce your taxable estate, or reallocating your assets to an even greater income bias.[4]

In these examples you can see short term, intermediate and long term financial goals that constitute a rough draft of your financial plan.

One more factor that will determine the success or failure of your financial plan is whether or not both spouses agree to abide by the set goals. If you are really excited about achieving the goals and your spouse is not, the spending will just be shifted from one area to another.

Financial Independence The ultimate goal is financial independence. All investors typically start out in a state of floundering. You are financially floundering when you don't have a financial plan or if you have a plan that doesn't work. In this stage people believe that as they make more money they'll be able to save more. Unfortunately, without a financial plan this never seems to happen, because in this stage people go on living from paycheck to paycheck, and finding new ways to spend any wage increases. Far too many people remain stuck in this stage. They're the ones who live out their final years in poverty, dependent on family or the Social Security system.

Once you have a workable financial plan in place, you are beginning to have some financial direction in your life. You've laid out a plan that eventually will generate enough income to support your basic life expenses. Those basic expenses include monthly mortgage payment or rent, utilities, food costs, insurance premiums, transportation costs, and property taxes. They don't include gifts, travel, or outside entertainment.

After years of disciplined savings following your financial plan, you can begin to reap the rewards of your sacrifices. At this point your portfolio provides enough interest income to pay for basic needs. This stage can be accomplished in as little as ten years, but you must have the discipline to start saving 15% of your income, and ideally increase your savings rate by 5% each year until you are saving 35%. At first, adjusting to the new spending level will be difficult. Fortunately, the longer you do it, the easier it gets.

As you continue your savings program (which you have discovered is quite natural by now) you will eventually achieve financial independence. You'll know when you have achieved financial independence because one day you'll wake up and realize that it doesn't matter one way or another if you go into work. You are secure in the realization that your portfolio is generating enough interest income to support every aspect of your lifestyle. Then you will have begun living my definition of retirement. A retired person does what he or she wants without worrying about money. You can work for charity. You can travel as much as you want. You can get a degree in philosophy. Or you can continue working in your current profession, if you enjoy what you do. Being retired, or financially independent, gives you that choice.

Ron   Who says old engineers just become obsolete and quietly and sedately fade away? Certainly not Ron. He is a vital, youthful 64-year-old engineer who has outlasted three changes in company ownership in the past three years. "Stability in management is one thing, and stability in engineering is something else. To have true stability in anything, you have to keep your options open and stay one step ahead of the game," he says.

Good advice, but not something he has always applied to his own life. Though he was ahead in his professional life, financially he was falling dangerously behind. He saved nothing for retirement because he believed that it would be taken care of by the government and his company pension.

At age 54 he realized he was floundering financially. Retirement was only 10 years away and he was not ready. He panicked. He couldn't rely on a company pension because of the instability in his profession. One more change in the company, or any kind of income interruption at his age would have been fatal to his retirement plan.

He sought professional investment help and was referred to me by a client who had already achieved financial independence. It was obvious that he needed to build a substantial portfolio fast. At the time, he stated, "All my life I've worked hard for what I got, and I enjoyed the life my earnings made possible. The problem is now I am nearing the end of my income earning years. If I had implemented a regular savings plan years ago, I would not be in this situation. What really scares me is that in the next ten years I need to create a source of income that will last for many more years. On the face of it, I'm not sure that is possible."

While Ron was correct in assuming that he should have started earlier, a secure retirement was still possible. He had two things that would help. First, he felt a sense of urgency which would enforce his need for discipline. Second, his salary was $50,000 and he had few expenses. Though he hadn't saved a lot of money, he had always paid cash for his cars and had no debts.

Ron's family's portfolio was approximately $70,000. He had $35,000 in his 401(k) plan. In addition, after her dad's death, Ron's wife had inherited $35,000 after probate, legal expenses and Uncle Sam's greedy cut.

Using a simple formula of wealth accumulation, Ron determined that he would need a $315,000 portfolio to support his basic needs: monthly home or rent payment, utilities, food, insurance, transportation and property taxes. (Note that we did not adjust for inflation; the issue of inflation will be addressed in Chapter 7.) Ron's monthly expenses were:

Home	$ 1,000	per month
Utilities	$ 300	per month
Food	$ 350	per month
Insurance	$ 150	per month
Transportation	$ 50	per month
Property Taxes	$ 250	per month
Total	$ 2,100	per month
x	12	Months
	$25,200	Required Annual Income

The next step was to divide the required income figure by 8%, an assumed rate of return. The result, $315,000 was the amount needed to support his basic needs. At this point, Ron finally had some direction in his financial life.

Next, he committed to saving 15% of his income every year and increasing that figure 5% annually until he was saving 35%. We set up the following schedule for the next eight years.

Age	Current Portfolio Size	Annual Portfolio Income	Ron's Annual Income	Percentage of Income Saved	Ron's Annual Savings	Ending Portfolio Balance
56	$ 70,000	$ 5,600	$50,000	15 %	$ 7,500	$ 83,100
57	83,100	6,648	52,500	20	10,500	100,248
58	100,248	8,020	55,125	25	13,781	122,049
59	122,049	9,763	57,881	30	17,364	149,176
60	149,176	11,934	60,775	35	21,271	182,381
61	182,381	14,590	63,813	35	22,334	219,305
62	219,305	17,544	67,003	35	23,451	260,300
63	260,300	20,824	70,353	35	24,623	305,747

Due to a good run in the financial markets, we were able to generate a 12% annualized return over this period. That allowed Ron to become financially secure a year ahead of schedule, by age 62. Today, Ron's portfolio is valued at over $370,000, about $65,000 ahead of our goal and he plans to work for one more year. By the time he retires, his portfolio should be worth over $500,000. In addition, his monthly expenses will decrease by $1,000 when he turns 67, as his house will be paid for. The extra $12,000 a year will make a big difference, almost 50% of his basic needs. The way Ron figures it, he will be financially independent.

After eight years of disciplined savings Ron is much more at ease with his life. He reflects, "The first few years were hard. My family and I were used to spending the money we should have saved. We had a few lapses, believe me. But we kept our goal in mind and it got much easier."

He summed up his experience, with some advice. "Don't wait. Develop a plan to build your portfolio to the point that it will take care of your basic needs. Stick to it. It will be difficult, but the end result is well worth it."

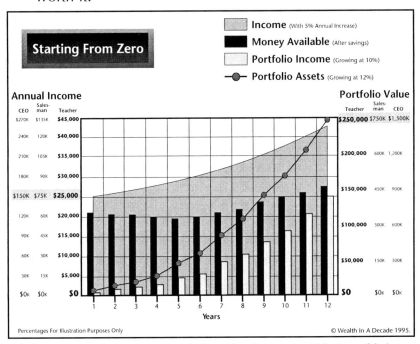

Whether you are a teacher, a salesman, or a chief executive officer, you can still fund a portfolio large enough to support your basic needs in around 10 years. It's not magic, however; you must have the discipline to start saving 15% and adding any salary increases to your savings.

The Bottom Line

- Accept that it is possible to achieve financial independence in ten years.
- Stop floundering financially: Set financial goals and create a financial plan.
- Include in your plan all your goals as well as the portfolio size you need.
- Commit to saving at least 15% of your income and increasing that percentage annually.
- Begin now.

Chapter 1

Exercise 1

Only include your very basic needs in this exercise. We will build on this amount in later chapters, however to avoid sticker shock and to demonstrate that this is possible, keep to the basics.

	BASIC NEEDS	You	Ron
A.	Shelter (Home/Rent)	$_____ /mo	$ 1,000 /mo
B.	Utilities (Electric/Gas/Water/...)	$_____ /mo	$ 300 /mo
C.	Food (Grocery Store Items)	$_____ /mo	$ 350 /mo
D.	Transportation (Car/Bus)	$_____ /mo	$ 50 /mo
E.	Insurance (Health/Life/...)	$_____ /mo	$ 150 /mo
F.	Taxes (Property/Car Tabs/...)	$_____ /mo	$ 250 /mo
G.	Other (Must Be Basics)	$_____ /mo	$ 0 /mo
H.	**Total Monthly Needs** (A+B+C+D+E+F+G)	$_____ /mo	$ 2,100 /mo
I.	Calculate Annual Income Needed	x 12	x 12
J.	**Total Annual Income** (H multiplied by I)	$_____ /year	$ 25,200 /year
K.	Assume 8% Return On Portfolio	.08	.08
L.	**Portfolio Size Required to Support Basic Needs** (J divided by K)	$_____	315,000

Exercise 2

Legend:

(a) Assume 8% return on your portfolio.

(b) Apply what reflects your own situation; for Ron we assumed a 5% increase in annual income.

(1) Continue to add 1 to your age as you move down the table.

(2) Start with what you currently have in investments (this could be zero), and as you move down the rows, this should be the same number that is in the Year End Portfolio Size (column 7) from the previous row.

(3) This is a straight calculation, multiply the Current Portfolio Size (column 2) by the % return on your portfolio (see Legend item a).

(4) Enter the income you anticipate over the next ten years.

(5) Enter the percentage of your income that you are willing to save each year. Make it a percentage that is possible. A good target is 15% and then work your way up to a percentage that will allow you to achieve your goals.

(6) Multiply the Family Annual Income (column 4) by the % Of Income Saved (column 5).

(7) Add "Current Portfolio Size" (column 2) and "Annual Portfolio Income" (column 3) together with "Dollars Income Saved" (column 6) to determine this amount.

(1) Your Age	(2) Current Portfolio Size	(3) Annual(a) Portfolio Income	(4) Family(b) Annual Income	(5) % Of Income Saved	(6) Dollars Income Saved	(7) Year End Portfolio Size
56	$70,000	$5,600	$50,000	15%	$7,500	$83,100
57	$83,100	$6,648	$52,500	20%	$10,500	$100,248
___	___	___	___	___	___	___
___	___	___	___	___	___	___
___	___	___	___	___	___	___
___	___	___	___	___	___	___
___	___	___	___	___	___	___
___	___	___	___	___	___	___
___	___	___	___	___	___	___

Footnotes

1   Silva Method — Silva International, Inc., Jose Silva, 1110 Cedar, P.O. Box 2249, Laredo, TX 78041

3   Creating Wealth, Robert G. Allen, Simon & Schuster, 1983, 1986, page 23

4   The Consumer Reports Money Book, by Janet Bamford, Jeff Blyskal, Emily Card, Aileen Jacobson and the Editors of Consumer Reports Books, Consumer Reports Books, 1992, page 116 - 117

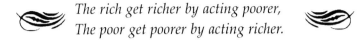

The rich get richer by acting poorer,
The poor get poorer by acting richer.

Chapter Two
The Law of Frugality

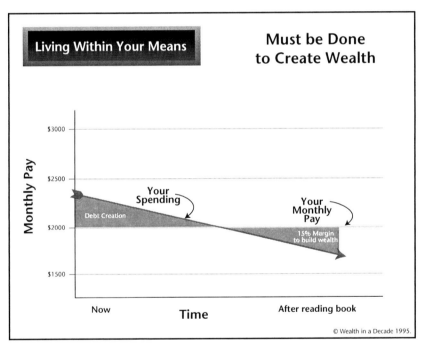

Becoming wealthy is more a function of what you spend than what you make. After you read this book, you should be starting a program designed to eliminate your debt and begin spending less than you make.

To be frugal is to practice moderation, restraint, prudence, thrift, and financial equilibrium, but it certainly isn't being miserly or stingy. Robert Louis Stevenson must have known something, because despite lifelong health problems, being married, traveling widely, and writing a lot, he described frugality like this: "To live a little and to spend a little less."

This step is simple and it's one of the most abused and misconstrued of the Ten Laws. Basically, the point is to spend less than you make in order to achieve financial independence.

To be able to spend less than you make, you have to know how much you spend and on what. Many of us amble through life with absolutely no idea where our money goes, and have never thought of tracking our spending habits for a few months to see how we spend our hard-earned resources. The reason many don't try to track their spending habits is because they don't think it's possible to track every penny. I don't either. Besides, it's stressful to have to remember to write down the nickel you gave to your child for the gum machine or the 37 cents you gave to Jerry's Kids at the 7-Eleven. While these small expenditures can and do add up, tracking them simply isn't worth the effort. Generally, I recommend that if it costs less than a dollar, forget it.

One exception to this rule is that you need to pay attention if you're consistently buying something that costs less than a dollar. For example, every day I bought a can of mineral water out of the soda machine at the office. Then the idea hit me to bring water from my water purifier at home. It tastes better, I know it's pure, and for the past several years I've saved about $125 a year. At 8%, that yearly savings would grow into enough money to buy a luxury car in 35 years. All that just from bringing water from home!

While it's fun to look at projections like that, for most people that $125 a year would never be seen. It would simply be absorbed into the spending patterns of day to day life.

The key to success with frugality is to have a reward for your sacrifice. If you consciously choose to give up something, you must make sure that you have the discipline to invest the savings. Otherwise, frugality will just provide you with more money to spend.

In order to identify areas that savings can come from, your expenses will have to be tracked. I realize that idea of tracking all of your expenses is not one that most people find very inviting. It will take some time and a great deal of self discipline. It may cause some tension in the family. I've heard discussions that went like: "Well, if you didn't spend all of that money on your fishing equipment..." or "You buy a new pair of shoes every two weeks!" The object is not to place fault. In most instances of over-spending, all family members have contributed to the condition. Rather than pointing fingers, try to identify how everyone involved can help cut expenses, even the kids.

I'm not going to pull any punches here. The seemingly simplistic idea of knowing how you spend your money is the most critical concept necessary to becoming wealthy. Remember, my research indicates that it's not what you make, it's what you spend that determines how wealthy you will become. There are as many CEO's that are living paycheck to paycheck as there are secretaries. Therefore, CEO's will need to track their expenses as well.

The idea behind tracking expenses is to identify those areas that take a disproportionate percentage of income. One woman called me after attending one of my seminars and said that she discovered that she and her husband spent over $5,000 a year for dining out. Another couple I met with found out that they had been spending over $800 a year on their morning coffee, because they each bought a cup of coffee downtown every day before work. These examples illustrate some of the many areas in our spending habits that can be trimmed considerably, while not detracting from comfort.

My friend told me that he couldn't understand where all their money went. His and his wife's combined income was about $75,000. They lived in a new house with mortgage payments that were only about 25% of their income and that left a lot of available money. Where were the disappearing dollars? I advised him to track their spending habits for three months and then go over them with me.

After a month passed he called me. "Brett, we've discovered that we're taking 20% of our monthly take-home pay in the form of cash from the cash machine, 20%! We had no idea it was that much and have even less of an idea where it's going." At the end of the three months, they had compiled enough information to make an accurate cash flow analysis. The ATM withdrawals, which were used for impulse buying, were the item that consumed the third greatest amount of money after the mortgage payments and 401(k) savings. More often than not, people will buy something with cash when they wouldn't buy it with credit cards or checks because cash is faster and more convenient. I recommended that they give themselves a weekly allowance and make a trip to the cash machine only every Friday. Consequently, they write more checks now and that makes it much easier to track their expenditures. As an added bonus, they are saving the fees the bank had instituted on cash machine withdrawals.

Begin by identifying those expenses that can be eliminated from your budget, while not reducing your current quality of life. These expenses are the things you no longer enjoy or, in most cases, don't enjoy as much as you once did. Remember, for every item, activity or expense on your list, there's a less expensive but essentially equal alternative. Often the only change is a brand name and the difference won't be noticeable. If you feel deprived, look again at your goal: financial independence.

Commonly, people have discovered that it's unnecessary to have the perpetual car payment they get by taking out a new three- to five-year car loan as soon as the old one is paid off. Something as simple as driving the same car for a few years after it's paid off can free up to $500 a month which can be added to savings. In 15 years, adding $500 a month to savings at 8%, you could buy a car with some of the annual interest on your portfolio. This is just one area of unnecessary expenses that my seminar attendees have discovered when they gave it some thought. Other unnecessary expenses they've mentioned include:

- Dining out excessively when they can designate one day a week as "Dine Out Day."
- New clothing purchases when it is just as easy to buy clothing on sale and to eliminate the need for the latest fashions. They'll be out of style soon enough.
- Extravagant vacations, when they can stay at budget or mid-priced hotels rather than luxury hotels.
- Going to movie theaters when they could wait for the soon-to-come video.
- Furnishing a home all at once when they could buy a piece at a time as money is available.

When you think about your spending, you'll find many hundreds more ways to cut corners, not quality of life.

Remember that you must reward yourselves for these temporary sacrifices by investing the savings. A savings of only $1.00 a day grows to over $215,000 over a 43 year working lifetime at 10% interest. That translates into over $1,400 a month in interest income at retirement. If you are even slightly more aggressive and save $5.00 a day, at 10% interest you'll accumulate over $1,000,000 by the time you're ready to retire. That's just $5.00 a day! Many people could save this amount by taking the bus to work or eating out a few less times a month. These examples show that wealth is attainable for almost all income levels. The rewards for disciplined savings from often unnecessary luxuries can be immense over a lifetime.

Another method of saving money is turning an expense into an income. For example, I began doing aerobics in 1981 to keep fit. After two years of paying health club dues, I decided to start teaching aerobics. That way, I am getting paid instead of paying for doing what I love. Getting paid about $90 a week couldn't make me rich. Or could it? If I invested that $90 a week at 8%, it would grow to over $2 million by the time I retire. If you turn something that you are currently paying for but love doing into a part-time job, you could do the same thing.

Here are some additional money saving ideas in common spending areas that I've discovered over time:

House   A home is the biggest single investment that most people will probably ever make. There are some ways to save money on purchasing a house. You may be able to save thousands of dollars in real estate agent commissions if you do some of the work yourself. For example, you may be able to work out a reduced commission if you agree to find a buyer yourself. You will still get the agents expertise and assistance in the other areas of the deal.

Another way to save money when buying a house is to avoid buying more house than you really need. Lenders, of course, want you to take out the biggest mortgage that you possibly can — around 28% of your income. If you buy a house with a mortgage payment that is only 20 or 25% of income, you will have a lower payment albeit on a slightly smaller home. You will also save money on furnishings, upkeep, and property taxes.

After you have bought your house and are paying off your mortgage, you can avoid a great deal of interest expense by making one extra full mortgage payment at the beginning of every year. If you follow this strategy, you may be able to cut your mortgage repayment time in half.

Cars   The biggest money saving trick to buying a new car is to not buy a new car. The average car loses about 33% of its value in the first three years[1], even though you can expect it to run well for many more years, especially with prudent upkeep. Certain models depreciate less and some much more. Consumer magazines often offer a depreciation index on used cars. Buying a two or three-year-old car provides the maximum combination of price and expected life. Some dealers even sell certified used cars that include an extended warranty.

Used cars have become even a better deal in recent years because of good quality cars that are returned at the end of their leases. Dealers faced with so many cars coming back are eager to offer a good deal.

The best deals on comparable cars are often found by buying out of the newspaper, rather than from a dealership, as long as you remember there's no recourse if something goes wrong with the car. Always check the Wholesale and Retail Blue Book to find out the value of the car you want to buy, using the wholesale bluebook when buying from the newspaper, and the retail bluebook when buying from a dealer. Banks or credit unions have the Blue Books for your specific area of the country. Car values in the book will differ by geographic area, so be sure to check a local edition.

Some people are absolutely determined to buy a new car. In that case, Consumer Reports has a telephone service that gives a comparison between the sticker price and the actual dealer invoice price. Unlike any other service, Consumer Reports bases its prices on the geographic location of the car because it relies on the caller's zip code. This service can save buyers hundreds of dollars and levels the playing field between car dealers and consumers.

When it comes to paying for the new car, there are three choices: cash, financing and leasing. Cash is always the cheapest option, but it is not always practical for younger buyers. In that case, financing is usually the next cheapest alternative. Shop around for the loan. There are often substantial differences between dealership, bank, and credit union financing. Finally, while leasing sounds attractive and accounts for nearly 25% of all new car sales[2], it's often not a good deal because lease agreements aren't standardized. This means that all the figures you need to make an informed decision may not be disclosed. However, if you must get a new car every year, don't drive a lot of miles and, if you take the time to study the lease contract, leasing may be your best bet.

Travel One of the biggest ways to save money on travel is to go during off-peak seasons. Broadly speaking, peak travel times are defined as Memorial Day to Labor Day. Many times, for example, it's possible to get an ideal vacation in a tropical location in September or May. An added benefit of off-peak travel is that it's less crowded. While off-peak travel may not be practical with children, it should be explored as an option whenever possible.

Another source of large travel savings is taking charter trips. Charters use passenger volume to create big discounts in airfare, hotel and ground transportation. While charters may not book the best hotels and don't always use big name airlines, they go to the same places often for a fraction of the price.

Debt   A discussion of frugality wouldn't be complete without spending some time on debt, specifically credit card and installment debt. It would be nice if all readers of this book were debt free, but my research indicates a much different story. An overwhelming majority of my younger friends and associates have five or six credit cards and are carrying a debt load as high as 40% of their take-home paycheck.

For the vast majority of people, one credit card is all that is necessary. There is no need to have a Master Card, Visa, two department stores, and a gasoline card. You can use the same card at all of those locations. In most instances, the gimmicks or free-bees that most department stores or gasoline cards offer are more than offset by the high annual fees that they charge. Some general rules of thumb for credit card use: Obviously, the best policy is to pay off the balance every month. If you do this, make sure that you are using a credit card that charges no annual fee. If you are carrying a balance, make sure that you have a card that is charging the lowest rate of interest possible.

Still, one of the quickest ways I've found to get started on the right financial path is to simply cut up all unnecessary credit cards. If debt is left to fester, what often happens is that after months or years of chipping away at this debt, average people just give in and end up spending more than before. Finally, financial pressures overtake them and opportunities for meaningful investment are lost. Some have even experienced severe stress and its resulting health problems, divorce, and bankruptcy.

Being in debt is contrary to the whole concept of spending less than we make. It's like noticing you are overweight and deciding to ease off eating and get your body back in balance. Financially speaking, when you have credit card and install-ment debt, you need to ease off spending and get your finances back in balance. Maybe getting them in balance for the first time ever.

Is there a way to go on a spending diet that will work? In a word, yes. It is possible to eliminate debt and start a healthy savings process. It takes time and self-discipline, and having a plan helps enormously. No true savings can happen until debt is eliminated. One of the best models of debt reduction I've found is included in the exercises at the end of the chap-ter.

Ross   While the term "Catch 22" doesn't quite apply to Ross, it comes pret-ty close. He's 22-years-old and doesn't know which way he wants his life to go. He has several choices: marriage, graduate school, a job, and deciding where to live. Instead of making a choice, he could just kick back and let his life find its own course. While Ross isn't sure what exactly he wants, he has already made one choice that will help him throughout his life no matter what he decides to do: He's decided to live frugally.

"One of the things that helped me to understand the need to save money was my upbringing," says Ross. "I was brought up by my mother in a small town in South Dakota. Dad died when I was nine years old. No father and a small town job market for my mother meant that we had to get by on less for many years. Some of the things we did to save money back then, I still do today. For example, we were able to eat out maybe twice a month, so it was a big treat, even if we went to McDonald's. We had the same modest but dependable car for many years. I've never been able to understand spending $40,000 on a car when $15,000 will buy one that will get you from point A to point B just as easily."

When I first met Ross he was 18 and had just begun college. He claimed he had only one asset. In reality he had several, not the least of which was the common sense to separate fact from fancy. He also had strong values of sincerity, responsibility and strong religious and family ties.

The asset that Ross had referred to was cash. He had nearly $20,000. His mother had parlayed his $10,000 share of his father's life insurance into that sum by investing in CD's during the high interest rates of the 1980's.

Ross and I talked occasionally during his first couple years of college. What I expected to find was a young man tempted into spending a large amount of money that should have been used to pay for his last few years of college. He never did. Instead, he graduated with honors and a degree in finance.

"I was tempted to spend my college money on more than one occasion," he says. "But, looking back, I think the lesson that I could buy a toy if I wanted to, but didn't have to, had more of an effect than I knew. I learned to do without in the present in order to have more later. As long as I was in control of the decision, I felt comfortable, even if others had more things."

Ross ended his college years with around $10,000 in the bank, because he had worked summers to help pay for his education. At this time he has a 10 year old car that runs well and has decided to act on a couple of his choices. He plans to find a job and is engaged to a woman he met at college. To best conserve his cash, he has put $7,500 in a money market account with check writing privileges and the rest in his checking account. He has started a systematic savings program, taking $100 out of his checking account every month and investing it in a long term growth mutual fund. He credits this decision to his studies of finance.

"I think that living on less and saving for the future are vital. If I don't take the responsibility for my financial future, no one else will," he concludes.

The Bottom Line:
- Spend less than you make.
- Track your spending for at least three months.
- Eliminate unnecessary expenses.
- Stretch your dollar in cars, trips, purchases.
- Reduce your debt using a reduction plan.

Chapter 2

Exercises

Use these exercises to determine the best plan for you. It is important to review this information in detail in order to make the best decisions. We will be going through four steps outlined below. At the conclusion of these exercises you will know that wealth is not how much you make, but rather how much you spend.

1. Determining Where It All Goes
2. Identifying Opportunities By Listing Expenses In Descending Order
3. Minimizing Waste In The Budget
4. Eliminating Debt

> *"The wise man saves for the future, but the foolish man spends whatever he gets."*   Proverbs 21:20

Don't skip these exercises. If you cannot complete these, get help. Don't let your fears and embarrassment stop you from being wealthy in a decade. Places to go for help are your banker, accountant, financial planner, investment advisor — someone who will spend the time to help you put this together and help you help yourself.

1.) Determining Where It All Goes (Convert To Monthly
Amounts)

EXPENSE SUMMARY MODEL

EXPENSE ITEM	MONTHLY AMOUNT
Shelter (Mortgage / Rent)	
Household Utilities	
Household Expenses	
Food / Grocery Store Items	
Clothing	
Transportation	
Entertainment	
Gifts/Charitable contributions	
Allowances	
Insurance	
Credit card payments	
Other known monthly loan payments	
Publications (newspapers, books magazines, audio)	
Vehicle tax, licenses, insurance	
Property tax, insurance	
Christmas fund	
Household furnishings / decorating	
Vacation	
Other quarterly, annual, yearly expenses	
TOTAL MONTHLY EXPENSES	
TOTAL TAKE-HOME INCOME (PAY)	
NET SAVINGS (Income - Expenses)	

2.) Identifying Opportunities By Listing Expenses In Descending Order — List from the largest monthly expenditures to the smallest, the top seven monthly expenses.

Dollars   Expense

_____   _____

_____   _____

_____   _____

_____   _____

_____   _____

_____   _____

_____   _____

3.) Minimizing Waste In The Budget — The following are suggestions for reducing or minimizing expenses. Check to determine if there are any items which are impractical or unnecessary. Determine which you are spending money on that could be eliminated and still allow you to maintain your present quality of life.

__ Are you maintaining and insuring a vehicle that you rarely drive?

__ Can you park a block further away from work and reduce parking costs?

__ Could you ride the bus or car pool to work rather than drive?

__ Do you really watch those premium cable channels?

__ How much do you plunk into vending machines (pop, snacks, etc.), and could you purchase it elsewhere for less and bring it to work with you?

__ Can you bring to work a lunch from home?

___ Is your ATM a non-descript hole of money (begin to track it)?

___ Can you drive that auto one more year?

___ What services do you purchase that could be done by yourself or possibly less frequently (outside laundry, house cleaning, yard work, etc.)?

___ How often do you dine out, and could it be just as pleasurable, or even more, if it were reduced?

___ What about purchasing used sports equipment?

___ Are your insurance policies with one agent that offers a discount?

___ Have you reviewed your auto policies (deductibles, special riders, limits - if you have an umbrella policy)?

___ Do you buy clothing only when on sale?

___ Do you make your kids pay the added costs of designer clothes?

___ Is your hair stylist really worth the cost — if so, is it possible to reduce the number of visits, or alternate with a less expensive service provider?

___ If you are constantly carrying a balance on your credit cards, put them away until they are cleared up, and then only use them sparingly.

___ Have you checked with your energy provider company to see if they have an energy savings plan that you can participate in with little or no impact to your comfort?

Now apply what you can to your updated expense summary model.

EXPENSE SUMMARY MODEL (Convert All Expenses To Monthly Amounts)

EXPENSE ITEM	MONTHLY AMOUNT
Shelter (Mortgage / Rent)	
Household Utilities	
Household Expenses	
Food / Grocery Store Items	
Clothing	
Transportation	
Entertainment	
Publications	
Gifts / Charitable contributions	
Allowances	
Insurance	
Vehicle tax, licenses, insurance	
Property tax, insurance	
Christmas fund	
Household furnishings / decorating	
Vacation	
Other quarterly, annual, yearly expenses	
TOTAL MONTHLY EXPENSES	
TOTAL TAKE-HOME INCOME (PAY)	
NET SAVINGS (Income - Expenses)	

4.) Eliminating Debt[3]

   a. The debts you want to target first are any stressful debts, short-term debts and high-interest rate debts. List these. Don't consider home mortgage, low-interest loans, and most car loans.

   b. Add them up.

   c. What average rate of interest do you estimate you're paying on these loans, 9%, 15%, 21%?

   d. To estimate how much you have available to pay off these debts, figure the minimum payment you make on each loan, plus interest.

   e. Divide the payments from question four, above, by the total debt from question two, and multiply by 1000.

   f. On the Debt Payoff Planner chart below, find the approximate number of months required to pay off your debt.

   g. Work with the chart and your budget until you find a payment schedule that you can live with.

   h. Increase your monthly payment to the amount you show in question seven. Pay off the highest rate loans first, and maintain at least minimum payments on all the other loans. That doesn't change the total months to pay off all debts.

   i. As you reduce your debts, turn the money you would have spent back to yourself by putting it into your savings.

   j. List your debts below and use the table to create a payoff schedule.

Debt	Amount Owed	Interest Rate	Minimum Payment	Targeted Payment	Payment $ per $1,000 of Debt	Months to Pay Off
_____	$_____	_____%	$_____	$_____	$_____	_____mos.
_____	$_____	_____%	$_____	$_____	$_____	_____mos.
_____	$_____	_____%	$_____	$_____	$_____	_____mos.
_____	$_____	_____%	$_____	$_____	$_____	_____mos.
_____	$_____	_____%	$_____	$_____	$_____	_____mos.
_____	$_____	_____%	$_____	$_____	$_____	_____mos.

Debt Pay-Off Planner: Interest Rate:

To Pay off $1,000 in this many months:	Pay Monthly	9%	15%	21%
	$20	63 mos.	79 mos.	120 mos.
	$25	48	56	69
	$30	39	43	51
	$35	32	36	40
	$40	28	30	33
	$45	24	26	28
	$50	22	23	25
	$60	18	19	20
	$70	15	16	17
	$80	13	14	14

For Example: If you owe $15,000 at 9% and you want to pay it off in two years, follow the 9% column down to 24 months = $45 x 15(thousand)= $675/mo.

Footnotes

1   Consumer Reports, April 1995, page 230

2   Consumer Reports, April 1995, page 268

3   Personal interview with Robert A. Ortalda, Jr., CPA, Fall 1995.

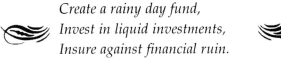

Create a rainy day fund,
Invest in liquid investments,
Insure against financial ruin.

Chapter Three
The Law of Liquidity

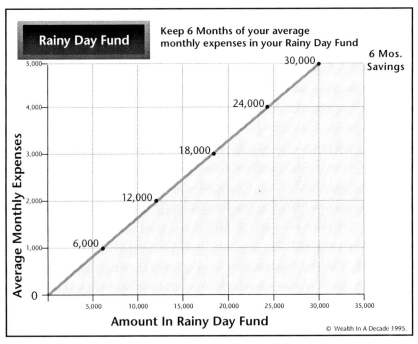

We recommend that everyone keep 6 months of their average monthly expenses in a rainy day fund. This fund is not considered a part of your portfolio, and should be invested conservatively in vehicles like money market funds.

The purpose of a rainy day fund is to avoid using portfolio monies when the inevitable unexpected expense arises. The possibilities of unexpected expenses are many: job loss, a divorce, an accident, illness, missed work, car break downs.

One of my clients had three financial emergencies happen on the very same day: his car's transmission broke, his home air conditioner stopped working, and the hot water heater burst and flooded his basement. This poor guy may have had a once-in-a-lifetime crisis, but these things don't always happen to the other person.

The day after all this calamity, he called saying that he needed $5,000 from his investment portfolio. Because he felt he always needed to be fully invested, I had to sell some securities in his account long before I would have liked and he had to pay commissions as well as watch his investment portfolio dwindle. Now, you guessed it, he keeps right around $5,000 in a money market fund for his next financial crisis.

The concept of the rainy day fund applies after retirement as well. Emergencies don't stop when you're drawing pension and social security. In fact, the number one cause of withdrawals from the portfolios of my retired clients is the need to provide financial support for their children. The loss of a job, a career change, a divorce or the loss of a second income due to the birth of a child are all examples of things that parents seem to end up paying for.

How much should a rainy day fund be? As a general rule, working as well as retired people should have six months of their average monthly expenses set aside.

Ideally, these funds will not be touched for long periods of time, so I recommend you put them where they will earn the most interest like in a money market account with check writing privileges. Money markets usually offer a yield advantage over similar short term investments. As with any interest bearing investment, shop around for the best yield. Don't leave your rainy day fund in your checking account.

The money earns very little interest and it's too easy to spend on day-to-day expenses.

Liquid Investments   The second part of the law of liquidity is to invest in liquid investments. That is, investments that are easy to liquidate if your personal situation, market conditions or tax laws change. Successful investors understand clearly the difference between liquid and non-liquid investments.

One of the best examples of a changing personal situation is simply growing older. As you grow older, you need to gradually shift your assets from equity investment to income producing investments. If part of your portfolio is tied up in liquid investments, this shift won't be possible and you will be deprived of income to live on. A sixty-year-old man came to me because he had nearly half of his portfolio locked up in limited partnerships or penny stocks that had stopped trading or were worthless. There wasn't much I could do for him except position the other half of his portfolio as best I could.

Another reason to maintain portfolio liquidity is to be ready if and when market conditions change. A good example is what happened in the early 1980's to the vinyl record industry. At that time, vinyl records had a majority of the market share in the recorded music industry. Along came compact discs and vinyl record sales plummeted to almost nothing in less than a decade. Those invested in industries benefiting from the manufacture of vinyl records stood to lose a lot of money, particularly if the investment was in the form of non-liquid securities issued by these manufacturers.

Finally, portfolios should be liquid to survive changing tax laws. One of the greatest examples of tax law changes affecting securities is what happened to the real estate limited partnership (LP). These securities were set up to take advantage of the tax laws that were in effect in the early 80s. Unfortunately, much of their appeal was wiped out by the Tax Reform Act of 1986, and their market dried up. A large percentage of the real estate LPs that were purchased in the early 80s cannot be sold today. If they can be sold, it's generally for a few cents on the dollar.

In sum, be aware of possible changes that can affect your investments. A current situation is the much-discussed income tax reform that is gaining support in Congress. If this kind of legislation is enacted, it's hard to tell what the effect will be on the municipal bond market. Will bonds lose their appeal to high-tax bracket investors? Only time will tell.

How liquid are the two most common investments, stocks and bonds? Traditionally, one of the most liquid investments available is common stock. Most exchange traded stocks can be sold immediately. That immediate availability becomes less when dealing with unlisted stocks traded over the counter. Some of these stocks, which are usually those of smaller companies, have very little trading volume or few shares outstanding, and they may not trade for days or even months.

Most bonds have a very active secondary market. This includes government bonds as well as highly-rated corporate and municipal bonds. Bonds that can suffer from a lack of liquidity include lower rated "junk" bonds, non-rated bonds and church bonds. For example, one client, prior to working with me invested in some bonds issued by a TV evangelist. She had about $250,000 or 30% of her portfolio invested in these bonds. When the evangelist filed for bankruptcy, she got back only 20 cents on the dollar and that only after a very long settlement period.

Insure Against Financial Ruin   The third part of the law of liquidity is to insure against financial ruin. Insurance is vital to make sure you are prepared in the event of an unrecoverable loss. While the purpose of this book is not to sell insurance, insurance is crucial to your financial well being. I recommend shopping around to get the best price and to find an experienced agent who will take the time to sit down with you to set up an overall insurance plan that may include home, auto, life, health, disability and long term care. He or she will help you to determine amounts of coverage and a deductible structure that you are comfortable with. Also, I strongly recommend that everyone get an umbrella policy because of the litigious nature of our society today. If someone trips over a crack in your sidewalk, there's a good chance you are going to be sued, and it won't be for a few thousand dollars. An umbrella policy covers where you might have gaps or limits in the liability coverage from your other insurance policies. A million dollars in coverage can cost as little as $100 dollars a year.

Here are a few general guidelines for each category of insurance. Become familiar with these guidelines before contacting an insurance agent.

When buying auto and home insurance, set the deductible as high as possible. This provides the greatest savings, and a high deductible will be no problem with a rainy day fund in place.

You should also have both policies issued by the same insurance company. In many cases you will get a discount for doing so. As an added benefit, you will only have to make one phone call when you need to report a claim. The agent can then determine which policy should pay for what. If you use different insurance companies for each policy, there may be delays in paying your claim because there will be finger pointing between companies as to who pays for what.

Evaluating life insurance needs is a key part of insuring against financial ruin, but how much and what kind is less clear-cut. For those who support a family, keep a household running, have a mortgage, or expect the kids to go to college, insurance can fill the financial gap left by death.

With no family or dependents, carry only enough life insurance to ensure a proper burial. On the other hand, if there are family or dependents, a simple rule of thumb is enough money to cover immediate cash needs and living expenses which is approximately seven to ten times the wage-earner's annual salary plus enough to pay off any out-standing debt including the mortgage. This will usually provide a portfolio that will pay enough income to provide for your family's needs.

However, a lot depends on individual lifestyle, number of dependents, and other sources of income. For example, let's say you have a salary of $50,000, current debt of $50,000 including mortgage, and a $100,000 liquid investment (those that can be easily and quickly converted to cash) portfolio. Based on this information, I recommend carrying $450,000 in life insurance. That's $50,000 salary times 10 plus $50,000 debt minus $100,000 liquid investments.

Try to use term life insurance versus the more expensive insurance policies, especially when following these guidelines. The idea behind term insurance in this application is that as we grow older, our need for life insurance decreases as our portfolio increases.

Avoid life insurance offered by the issuer of your mortgage. This insurance is designed to pay off your mortgage in the event of your death. It is often one of the most expensive forms of insurance available. You should include the mortgage in the amount of your main life insurance policy.

While most people take the time to set up some sort of life insurance, the average person doesn't have disability insurance. This often-overlooked coverage pays a monthly income if you are unable to work because of injury or illness. Statistics show that disability is far more probable than death, especially for the young or middle-aged. As a matter of fact, one out of every three individuals will suffer a long-term disability (extending an average of five years) prior to retirement.[1]

How much disability coverage? In general, I recommend that disability insurance coverage should equal approximately 70% of before-tax earnings. These benefits are paid tax-free and should start from 90 days to 6 months after disablement. Your rainy day fund will determine how long a waiting period is needed. There is a major difference in premium between the 90-day and 6-month waiting period. Benefits should continue until age 65 or until you can be retrained in another field providing the same level of income.

Also, the definition of disability, with respect to your current job is important. For example, if you are a heavy equipment salesperson earning $150,000 a year, will you still be covered if you can work at Sears Automotive Department selling drills at $16,000 a year? Most people don't know the conditions of their policy until it's too late. A good place to look for disability insurance is your employer, who is often able to offer disability insurance more cheaply because of group buying power.

The number one financial fear for my elderly clients is the cost of long-term health care. This is a non-stop expense that can quickly deplete resources built over a lifetime. If both husband and wife are in a nursing home at the same time, it's not unusual to see six or seven thousand dollars a month come out of the portfolio. At that rate, even a sizable portfolio can be paid down pretty quickly. Most Americans have done little, if anything, to prepare for the high cost of long-term health care.

Most people incorrectly assume that Medicare will pick up their nursing home bills. Medicare pays only for medical expenses incurred in skilled nursing homes, those staffed with doctors and nurses. That eliminates coverage for the majority of elderly patients who need custodial care only — help dressing, feeding and otherwise caring for themselves. And even for skilled nursing situations, Medicare pays only for the first 20 days in full, another 80 days of partial payments and no payments after 100 days.[2]

People under 50 may be best advised to do nothing about long-term care because broader and better solutions, public or private, may lie ahead in the not too distant future. But those past 50 can't afford to wait unless they have amassed a substantial, perhaps multi-million dollar, portfolio. Since the issue of long-term care policies is limited to those in good health, and the fact that few companies sell insurance to anyone over 80, it is prudent to have such insurance by age 70.

Ken   When East meets West, the result can be a success story. Take the case of Ken, who was born a long way from his current home in the Upper Midwest, USA. He was born in Japan, but his family relocated to the United States when he was seven. He recalls his growing up experiences as, "Not particularly memorable. I know I didn't come from a well-to-do family. We didn't have a lot. But I can't say I thought of myself as poor. I never lacked the necessities of life. I had shelter, food to eat, clothes to wear and a supportive family environment. Perhaps these are the key values we all need to learn during our formative years."

Were you to meet Ken on the street today, you'd see a typical professional person. Nothing stands out. He's conservatively dressed, and his mannerisms are quiet and reserved. He isn't an outgoing person who is easy to meet and get to know. On the job, he minds his own business and gets his work done. When not at work, he spends his leisure time with his wife and three-year-old daughter. Nothing particularly note-worthy. However, what may catch your attention is his meticulous attention to the needs of the people around him and his willingness to share his personal resources with the less fortunate. Ken attributes this demonstration of community responsibility to his Christian background, and the Oriental values of maintaining close ties to his nuclear family. He has retained these values and demonstrates them to the larger community family.

Because Ken values the security of his family so much, he has made sure that they are fully insured. He has good health insurance through his work. In addition, he increased his term life insurance cover-age to ten times his salary when his daughter was born. "It makes me sleep a lot better knowing that my family will be financially protected if something were to happen to me. A bit of advice with regard to life insurance: shop around. The difference in premiums I encountered was substantial," he says.

Ken also learned early the value of having a rainy day fund. He had been working for a couple of years and had accumulated almost no savings outside of his IRA account. Unfortunately, his here-to-fore reliable car blew an engine. It needed to be replaced immediately, as it was his only car. With no rainy day fund in place, Ken was forced to take a distribution from his IRA and pay a penalty and tax. "This was a painful way for me to learn this lesson. It's a lesson I won't need to relearn."

He began his rainy day fund shortly thereafter. He opened a money market account and began depositing $100.00 every month. He made sure the account had check writing privileges so that he could handle any more unexpected expenses quickly and easily.

After he had fully funded his rainy day account, he began investing in other securities. In the late 1970s he purchased a CD paying 11.75%. In 1981, he used the proceeds from it for a self-investment program: he paid his graduate school tuition with it. While pursuing his degree in health care, he expanded his investment program by selecting a series of liquid investments to begin his retirement savings. He purchased some large company common stocks and some U.S. Treasury zero coupon bonds. He has held these investments for several years and has taken advantage of compound interest. Today, he's 38 years old, has no debt other than his mortgage, and has a personal investment portfolio valued at about $50,000.

Ken's investment philosophy is to set priorities and be disciplined about sticking to them. He continues to build his money market balance through payroll deductions. When the account balance reaches a few thousand dollars over his rainy day fund needs, he transfers the excess into his brokerage account.

When he wanted to buy a house, Ken demonstrated proof of the power of cash. Ken says, "By 1986 I had saved enough to be able to offer a 20% down payment on a house that I liked. This qualified me for a more favorable mortgage rate and resulted in a lower monthly house payment and a savings on private mortgage insurance. With the difference between the rent we were paying and the mortgage, we were actually able to increase our monthly savings rate. Further, we got the tax benefit from the interest deduction, which got us a tax refund, another addition to our investment portfolio."

Both Ken and his wife believe in saving for retirement, especially when the government is subsidizing the cost by deferring taxation on any interest or capital gains. To prove his belief, Ken increased his withholding into his employer's 403 (B) plan.

Ken's case proves that spending, not income, determines wealth. At its existing rate of return, when Ken becomes 65, his current $50,000 portfolio will be valued at $1.65 million.

The Bottom Line

- Create a rainy day fund
- Invest in liquid securities
- Insure against financial ruin with home, auto, umbrella, term life, and long-term care insurance.

Chapter 3

Exercises

1.) Determining Your Rainy Day Fund
    A. How much is your take-home pay
        per month? _____
    B. Calculating rainy day fund level
        (A x 6 months) _____
    C. How much do you have in your rainy
        day fund? _____
    D. How much more do you need? (B - C)

  If you have less than six months take-home pay in your rainy day fund, set a goal to increase the fund to the proper levels soon as possible.

2.) Rule of Thumb for Determining Life Insurance Needs
    A. What is your yearly salary? _____
    B. Calculating life insurance level
        (A x 10) _____
    C. How much debt do you have (include
        mortgage)? _____
    D. What is the value of your liquid investments?
        (exclude retirement; include rainy day fund, and
        other investments) _____
    E. Insurance required (B + C - D) _____

3) Current Insurance Coverage

Company	Policy Amount
Employer Provided Insurance	_____
_____	_____
_____	_____
_____	_____
_____	_____
_____	_____
TOTALS	_____

How does your current coverage compare to what your estimated needs are? Make whatever adjustments are necessary.

    4.)   Recommended Disability Insurance Amount

    A. What is your yearly salary?   _____

    B. Calculating liability insurance fund
        level (A x .70)   _____

    C. How much insurance do you
        currently have?   _____

    D. How much additional insurance do
        you need (B-C)?   _____

The amount of insurance needed depends on many individual factors. These exercises are presented as general rule of thumb guidelines. Please consult a qualified insurance professional to help you determine your individual coverages.

If you don't have Long-term care insurance, find out how much it will cost given your specific health situation.

Footnotes

1   Wealth: How to Get It, How to Keep It, by Herb D. Vest CFP, CPA, CLU and Lynn R. Niedermeier CPA, CFS, AMACOM, 1994, page 48

2   Terry Savage's New Money Strategies for the 90's, by Terry Savage, HarperCollins, 1993, 1994, page 500

Chapter Four
The Law of Time Perspective

Patience and compound interest are two absolutely essential keys to wealth. Successful investors understand that wealth accumulation takes time, so they don't look for short term bonanzas. It's worth noting that some short term bonanzas do happen, but they're rare. In spite of all the talk they cause, a killing in the market is an anomaly. People who count on short term bonanzas to build their wealth stand an excellent chance of having to start building their portfolio all over again. Steady investing doesn't carry that risk.

Building wealth is not unlike raising a child. We begin with something small and vulnerable that, over the years, matures and grows into a self-sufficient being. Eventually, it could even end up taking care of the ones who originated it.

What exactly is the attraction of long-term investing? Two words: compound interest! Financier Baron Rothschild said, "I don't know what the seven wonders of the world are, but I know the eighth, compound interest." Successful investors understand this wonder and apply its power in every investment decision they make.

The story is told of how Manhattan Island was bought from the Manhattan Indians in 1626 for about $24 worth of beads and cloth. If that money had been invested at even a minimal rate of interest, it would now be worth enough to buy back the island of Manhattan.

Compound interest is truly amazing. If you were given $1.00 at birth and were able to double that dollar every year:

At age 15, you'd have enough money to buy a mid-priced car.

At age 18, you'd be able to buy a home valued at $130,000.

At age 22, you'd be earning $200,000 in interest from your investments if they were invested at 10%.

At age 30, you could own a $1 million dollar home in over 500 cities worldwide.

At just over 43 years of age, you would be able to pay off the national debt of approximately $5 trillion.

Just in time for retirement at age 65, you would have amassed the tidy sum of $18,000,000,000,000,000,000,000. I really have no idea what the name is for that amount of money. Suffice it to say that you could give about $72 billion to every man, woman and child in the United States (assuming a population of 250 million).

Why, if the power of compound interest is so wonderful and so readily available, doesn't everyone take advantage of it with their savings and investments? From my experience, the answer is that the average investor doesn't realize the advantages of starting to save early in life and letting the law of compound interest take over. They don't realize that, barring a complete collapse of the world's financial institutions, they could become wealthy by beginning a regular investment program when they got out of college.

Using the historical stock market rate of return of about 10%, you would only need to save $5.00 a day to accumulate a million dollars over the 43 years between college and retirement. The best way to harness the power of compound interest is to start saving as early as possible. If the person in the above example would have begun saving $5.00 a day upon starting college, he/she would have added another $600,000 to his/her nest egg. If the same person had been fortunate enough to invest $5.00 a day since birth, his/her portfolio would be worth over $9 million at age 65!

Rate of return also makes a major difference when dealing with compounding. By getting an additional 1% return over those 65 years (to 11%), the portfolio cited above would have grown to over $14 million. An additional 2% (to 12%) would have grown the portfolio to over $24 million.

I know of very few 22 year olds who, when presented with the possibility of being a millionaire in 45 years would not at least give saving some hard thought. Or better yet, I don't know of many parents who wouldn't start a savings plan at birth to really harness the power of long-term investing if they knew what the results could be.

Why then do I know so many 20-, 30-, 40- and even 50-year olds who have not yet begun a regular savings program? They've never learned the power of compound interest. Quite frankly, I believe that the concept of compound interest, as it applies to the financial markets, should be taught in high school and should be part of a required course in college. That way, at least people would be informed and could make the conscious choice of whether to save.

If the choice to save is made, the rule of 72 is a useful tool to show how different rates of interest, even small differences, can affect your portfolio. The formula involves simply dividing 72 by your rate of return. For example, at 7% it will take 10.2 years to double your money.

> That's   72 / 7 = 10.2 years.
> Or   72 / 6 = 12 years
>   72 / 8 = 9 years
>   72 / 10 = 7.2 years.

So if you make 6% on $100,000 dollars, in 12 years you'll have $200,000 dollars. If you can double your annual return to 12%, in 12 years you'll have four times as much or $400,000. If you can double that again and get 24% return, and not lose your money in the process, you can have eight times as much or $1.6 million after 12 years. Of course, I am not suggesting that you try for a home run and go for the 24% return. This is simply another illustration of the power of compound interest and how you can apply the rule of 72.

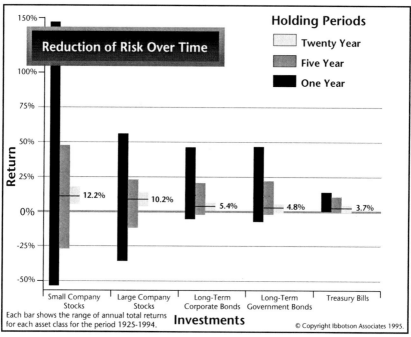

This graph shows the relationship between return volatility and time. Clearly, the longer an investment is held, the greater the chance of achieving positive returns. Even with small company stocks, whose one year total return range has proven to be amazingly large, a long time horizon reduced the risk associated with these stocks to an acceptable level.

While some investors are harnessing the power of compound interest, many more become disenchanted after a bad quarter in the stock market. For example, the average mutual fund holding is only nine months, far from long term. That kind of thinking causes the infamous buy high, sell low results that often plague individual investors. The average investor, after being invested in money market through the great majority of stock market run-ups, will eventually finally chase after the stock market and buy into stocks or mutual funds near the peak. Then after holding on for a few months of the inevitable pull back in stock prices, will take the money out of the market, usually at a loss.

Four Enemies of Proper Time Perspective Why is the average investor so short-sighted? I've identified four enemies of proper investment time perspective. The first one is hope, sometimes masquerading as stubbornness. "When the stock gets back to even, then I'll sell," is a typical statement of the hope-filled investor.

When the hope-filled investor buys a stock, he makes the purchase a measure of his intelligence. He researched the stock, so he's sure it will go up. But instead, the price slowly sinks into the sunset. Since the purchase was supposed to reflect his wisdom, he holds on. The stock, neither knowing nor caring whose intelligence it's supposed to reflect or how much it has to gain to break even, often responds by sinking further. The buyer has taken a magnificent loss. The average investor holds losing positions too long and sells gaining positions too quickly.

An associate who works for a full service brokerage firm told me about one of her clients who was determined to make all his investment decisions on his own. Typically, this type of investor is better off using a discount brokerage, as they offer cheaper commission rates than full service firms. She said it seemed that he was just using her services so that she would put her seal of approval on his stock picks. He would read about a stock in a financial magazine, call her up and say, "I read that XYZ Corp. is going to be at $50 in the next couple of months, what do you think?"

My friend would do an analysis of the stock or consult her company research and often was obliged to question the judgment of the pick. But he'd buy it against her advice and, more often than not, have to watch it go down. My friend, seeing her client's plight, would call him and recommend that he put a stop-loss order underneath the stock to limit his loss, but he'd stubbornly cling to his decision. His response was always the same, "I'm not sellin' until it gets back to even." Stubbornness has no place in the stock market.

On the other hand, I'm not recommending selling a stock blindly just because it's down. A decision to sell has to be based on information and consideration. If the fundamental reasons you bought the stock are breaking down, you should sell it. If, for example, you bought shares in a computer stock that just introduced a computer that would respond to your thoughts, and then the company announces that the computer will only respond if you sneeze, its probably a good time to sell the stock.

Conversely, if after a stock declines in price, the company announces no changes and the fundamentals are still in place, buy more of it. This often will happen during a normal market correction of 10% or more. Many times those shares that go up the fastest, go down the fastest as well during a correction. Those investors that have the conviction to buy these shares after a reduction in price are often richly rewarded.

The second enemy of proper time perspective is boredom. A bored investor might say, "I've been in the same stock for a whole year." Many stockholders just get tired of their stock when it's producing a steady total return of 10%, especially when they hear about how friends' shares of ABC Inc. went up 150% last year. If you look back at some of the greatest winners in the history of the stock market, you'll find many very good stocks that just plodded along year after year producing a steady total return. Some of them never had a big year when they gained 150%, but their gain in value was consistent.

Compare investments to the night sky: shooting stars and meteors are exciting to watch, but they burn out. The ones that shine on and on and on are the ones that give us a lifetime of comfort.

I use the degree of unrest in the bored individual investor to gauge how the stock market is valued. Usually near the end of a good gain in the markets, I start to get calls from my most conservative clients wondering why their portfolios are producing only a total return of around 10% when their friend at the coffee shop's portfolio of small company stocks is up 50%. At times like these, I advise my clients that the way to handle boredom is to stick to their overall investment strategy and predetermined risk tolerances.

The third enemy of proper time perspective is greed. Greed can be an extension of boredom. It's investors who want shooting stars all the time. A greedy investor might say, "I've already made 50% on my investment, but I know the stock will double." When the euphoria of watching a rising stock kicks in, it seems that it will go up forever. Instead, the darling-of-the-market stock drops five times faster than it went up, catching the greedy with what is known as a "round turn." That term depicts how a stock goes way up, creating huge paper profits, and then dives back to the purchase price, or lower.

A strategy that I often employ with investors of this mindset is to sell that portion of an appreciated stock position that is equal to what was paid for the whole position. For example, if you bought 200 shares of DEF, Corp. at $25, you paid around $5,100, assuming a 2% commission. Say that over several years the shares appreciate to around $52, and you sell 100 of those shares with a 2% commission. You will have locked in at least a 50% return regardless of what happens to the other 100 shares.

The fourth and final enemy of proper time perspective is fear. A frightened investor says things like, "The markets seem awfully high, I had better stick with CDs." or "The markets seem to go lower every day, I'd better stick with CDs." That's called trying to time, or predict, the market.

Fear costs investors more money than any other emotion. It keeps investors out of the right investments at the best times to buy. Studies have repeatedly shown that trying to time the market, the economy or interest rates is futile, no matter what "market timers" claim. If the direction of the stock market could be predicted correctly three or four times, one could become a billionaire. But there are few billionaires, which makes it pretty obvious that not many people have correctly predicted the direction of the stock market.

None of the top money managers around the U.S. with whom I've spoken attempt to time, or predict, the market. As a matter of fact, most of them believe that time in the market is more important than timing the market. A study conducted by the University of Michigan shows what can happen if you try to time the market. The study found that someone invested over the entire 1276 trading days of the 1980's bull market would have earned 26.3% annually if invested in the S&P 500. If that person had been trying to time the market and missed only the 10 days with the largest market gains, the return would have dropped to 18.33%. Missing the 20 largest gain days would have cut the return in half (13.15%), while missing the top 40 days (only about 3%) would have meant the return plunged to only 4.38%.[1]

Granted, it's not easy to invest bravely in a market that has been going up for several years, and it's no easier to invest in a market that has been going down for several years. In the case of a market that has been rising steadily for four or five years, many market observers begin to predict a market crash. That's what happened in the first half of 1995. The stock market had been rising gradually since the crash of October 1987 and talk was beginning to surface about another market crash. If average investors had listened to the experts, pulled their money out of the market and waited for that crash, they would still be watching the market rise as I write this. The point is, as long as you have a proper time perspective with relation to the type of investment you are looking at, there's always opportunity in some market.

A more painful situation results when dealing with a market that has been going down for several years. Many investors who have stuck it out are about ready to sell everything and put their money in a mayonnaise jar and bury it in the backyard. These discouraged investors tend to project the down trend for the foreseeable future. It certainly doesn't look like a good time to invest. But, this is truly an investment opportunity. Those investors who have the fortitude to plow money into the markets at down times often earn great rewards.

A related timing problem is unrealistic expectations, and sometimes, plain ignorance. Many novice investors buy a mutual fund just after it has an incredible year. In 1992 many investors bought into funds that had gone up 50, 60, 70% or more a year earlier, only to see them have a flat or negative return. One story is told of a customer calling one of the major fund companies at the end of 1992 and asking the customer service representative what exactly a mutual fund was and why her fund had lost money for the year. The representative explained mutual funds and told the caller that the majority of funds were flat in 1992 and that many had lost money. The customer said that she bought it because she thought mutual funds always went up.

Another aspect of time perspective is making sure that your investments match your time frame in terms of your overall financial goal. For example, if you accumulate $20,000 for a house down payment, and plan to buy the house in a year, you shouldn't invest in a stock mutual fund. Instead, invest in something that matures in a year and will preserve your capital, like a CD, Treasury note or zero-coupon bond. If, on the other hand, you're saving over 10 years for a house down payment, then a stock mutual fund would work well, or a ten-year bond for the more conservative.

What should a time horizon be for different investments? Hold stocks or other securities invested in stocks for at least three to five years. The longer you are in the stock market, the greater the chance of making money. If you need stock money in less than three years, there's a good chance that you'll have to sell at a loss. Bonds, CD's and other maturing investments should be held until they come due. In the case of some investments, like CD's or annuities, you may have to pay an early withdrawal penalty.

Joe   Joe knows the value of time. He uses every minute of his day to his advantage. As a result, he's busy and content. "I've never subscribed to the theory that you don't have time to do this or that. The bottom line is that you decide how to use your time. Everyone has the same amount of time, I just focus mine where it will most pay off in the long run. For proof that this concept works, I offer my excellent health, my happy wife and children, and my career."

Fortunately for Joe, he could also offer his investment portfolio. He has chosen to take advantage of the marvelous power of time and compound interest in his investing. So much so, that he started his kids out with a savings plan at birth.

In Joe's opinion the investment that pays the highest return is a college education. "Perhaps the best investment I can make is in the education of my kids. By doing so I help them to make an adequate living and stand on their own two feet."

He anticipated the day when tuition expenses for his children would arrive. He established social security numbers for each of his four children shortly after their birth, and opened savings and investment accounts under each social security number. While the children were young, any gifts of money that they received were deposited into their account. As they grew older and began to develop a need for money, he put half of the gift money into their account and let them keep the rest. "Sure they complained some as they got older, but when they saw how much money was accumulating in the account, they kind of enjoyed it. Over 18 years, with steady additions and a moderate rate of interest, even a small investment can turn into a large sum." A sum, in fact, large enough to pay for most of the tuition at a state college.

Following a regular savings plan also helped Joe increase his portfolio value from $10,000 twenty-five years ago to over $400,000 today. He calculates that over the years he added about $150,000, the rest being from interest and capital appreciation. Joe is a conservative "buy-and-hold" investor, capitalizing on stock splits, stock dividends, and cash dividends, all friends of long term investors. He works closely with me to find value in assets and quality in management. The result is $250,000 of portfolio appreciation. Not a bad payoff for an annual investment of $6,000.

If you can't set aside $115 each week into a savings plan, what can you afford to save? Perhaps said another way, how can you afford not to save something each week? How much time can you afford to wait before setting up a personal financial plan?

Joe has been working at his financial plan for 25 years. He offers the following advice to people just starting theirs: "Once you have constructed your plan, make a commitment to stick it out. It's going to be hard to keep adding to your portfolio at all times and even harder to keep your assets invested for the long haul." Joe adds, "Don't panic if the market crashes. I've lived through the last two major price breaks, and I've seen the market recover over time. If you've properly selected your stocks for their long term economic potential, their value will most likely recover."

Joe concludes, "If you don't have the time or ability to watch your investments for the long term, don't kid yourself. Seek the help of an investment professional. Ask your friends who they work with, if they're happy they'll let you know. If they're not, move on."

By taking a long-term, systematic approach to investing, and by committing to a cap on spending, Joe has built a portfolio that has him well down the road to becoming wealthy. He has also nearly ensured a college education for each of his four children. He's spending less than he makes. His portfolio is making money and he doesn't need for current expenses. In short, time is on his side.

The Bottom Line

- Invest for the long haul.
- Match investment to your time horizon.
- Have realistic expectations.
- Keep boredom, hope, greed and fear in check by committing to investment discipline.

Chapter 4

Exercises

Do your investments match your time horizon as to when you will need the funds? What are some expenses that you know will have to be prepared for? Recognizing these deferred spending items and including them in your expense summary model is a necessary part of developing wealth in a decade, because the expenses will come whether you are prepared for them or not.

Areas to consider:

— Vehicle purchase.

— Anticipated home improvement or down payment.

— College tuition for yourself or a dependent.

— Vacation home, travel, weddings, and other predictable large expenses.

DESCRIPTION	YEARS AWAY	AMOUNT REQUIRED	PRIORITY*	ESTIMATED MONTHLY AMOUNT
(example) 4wd sport utility (3yrs old)	3	$13,000	M	$333.70

*Priorities are categorized as High, Medium and Low.

Choose investments that will earn the best by the time you'll need the money. For example, for time horizons under three years, invest in maturing income securities like CDs or bonds, for investors over age 59 1/2, annuities. For time horizons longer than three years, phase into stock investments and look at greater percentages for longer time horizons.

Calculating the "ESTIMATED MONTHLY AMOUNT" is done using the following formula. The more exacting amount can be determined by using the NPV function on a calculator. For illustrative purposes and ease of computation this will be adequate for these exercises.

Calculating:
Estimated
Monthly
Amount

The following chart represents an 8% return on investment. If you wish to look at factors for other return rates reference the appendix - "Future Value Of Ordinary Annuity" table.

Year	Factor	Year	Factor
1	1.0000	6	7.3359
2	2.0800	7	8.9228
3	3.2464	8	10.6366
4	4.5061	9	12.4876
5	5.8666	10	14.4866

Example

A. Amount required _____ 13,000.00

B. Expense factor (from chart above)_____.___ 3.2464

C. Annual expense (C = A / B) _____ $4,004.44

D. Computed monthly expense
   (C/12) _____ $333.70

Footnote

1   A Guide to Growth Investing, (actual source University of Michigan Study), brochure, Smith Barney research, 1994, page 15

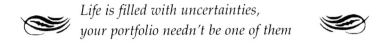

*Life is filled with uncertainties,
your portfolio needn't be one of them*

Chapter Five
The Law of Prudent Investing

Successful investing does not happen by fate, luck or chance. Growing wealthy through investing requires planning, prudence, insight, discernment and a moderate level of risk. The risk involved in investing induces caution. That's natural, even prudent, because risk is assumed every time you make an investment, even if you choose to put your money under the mattress. But risk shouldn't mean fear. If you're too conservative, you'll remain static financially or even lose money after taxes and inflation. If you're too aggressive, you can lose all of your investments and be forced to start the process of building a portfolio over again and again and again.

The main focus of the law of prudent investing is to avoid investments and investment schemes that expose you to substantially more risk than probability of increased return. Said another way, prudent investors avoid high risk investments, unscrupulous investment services, leverage, and strategies that promise to make a million overnight.

Prudence goes hand in hand with conservative investment strategies. I also believe you can be prudent when employing moderate investment strategies as well. Aggressive investing has no place in the prudent scheme of things. Most successful investors have built their portfolios over many years, and for the most part their investment plans are somewhere between conservative and moderate. While some successful investors have invested aggressively over the years, most aggressive investors are far behind where they might have been had they followed a steady, conservative or even moderate investment philosophy.

On the other hand, prudence is not synonymous with risk avoidance. For example, when another broker in our firm was leaving, he asked me to take over the portfolio of one of his clients, a 50-year-old man. I asked my new client to come to my office to discuss his goals, objectives and risk tolerances. When I pulled up his account on the computer, I saw there was about $300,000 in a money market fund. After we had talked for a while, I had a good idea about why the account was in cash: he didn't trust the government, and because the government regulated the financial markets, he hadn't put his money in anything but money market or savings accounts for over 30 years. Even after I explained to him that he had most likely lost money over that 30 year period due to taxes and inflation, he still refused to purchase any securities.

A couple of weeks later he telephoned. "Have I really been losing money for 30 years?"

"I'm afraid so," I said.

He asked if it was too late to try to change his situation. I assured him it wasn't, and gradually we eased him into some high-dividend stocks and, yes, some government bonds. It turns out that the only thing he was more afraid of than the government was losing money.

The reverse can also be a killer. A friend's experience is a painful example of what can happen if your investment strategies are too aggressive. Because he had been investing for many years, he was way up on the investment market letter mailing list. Four or five of these letters would send him a sample copy almost every week asking for him to subscribe and flaunting their performance. Finally, he gave in and decided to subscribe to a market letter that claimed to be very successful in picking foreign stocks. Just before the huge pullback in the foreign markets late in 1994, he sold a couple of his U.S. stock funds worth maybe $20,000 which comprised about 60% of his portfolio. He invested the proceeds in four of the foreign stocks recommended by the letter. Within a month he had lost $12,000. Clearly, he suffered from a case of bad timing, but just the same, his aggressive exposure to the foreign markets cost him dearly.

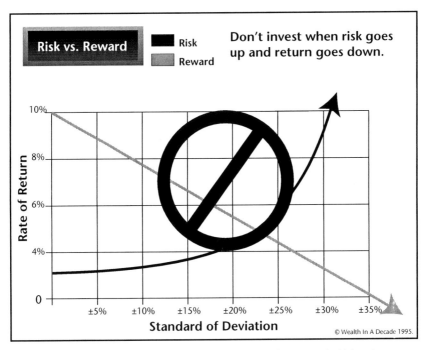

Certain investments offer more risk than they can consistently provide in return. Avoid these investments or at least limit them to 5% of the equity component of your portfolio.

Investing...or Gambling? There are certain "investments" out there that are little more than a gamble. Prudent investors avoid such investments, or limit them to 5% or less of the risk or equity component of their portfolio. There are hundreds of investments that have been created to lure investors with the prospect of getting rich quick. There has been much talk lately about derivatives, those investments that derive their value from the value of another security. Several bond mutual funds lost a great deal of money in 1994 because they were invested in derivatives. Why mess with something that even expert portfolio managers don't understand? You don't need any investment other than stocks, cash, bonds and other fixed income securities to become wealthy.

While some of these high-risk investments are so exotic that it would take several pages to even explain, I will stick to a discussion of three of the most common: penny stocks, commodities and options. These are examples of high-risk gambles and should be avoided by prudent investors.

Penny stocks are defined as common stocks with a market price at or below $5. They are issued by small or start-up companies, often with an erratic history of earnings, and are therefore more volatile than stocks traded on the large exchanges. Their shares are usually associated with exploration firms, mining companies and unprofitable firms that are in the process of going out of business.

Although the odds of success in penny stocks are relatively low, some of these troubled or fledgling companies do make good. America offers the opportunity for small companies to grow into big ones. As a consequence, many individual investors buy penny stocks hoping to get a huge return. They think that because they can buy a lot of shares they can earn a larger profit.

"It's only a buck," they say. "What can I lose?"[1]

A buck, that's what. And every other buck invested. All of it. No less easily than if you bought a $50 stock. A cheap per share price of $3 or 50 cents doesn't indicate a better deal. As with anything else, you get what you pay for. For example, once I bought a stock at $2.25 that traded up to $2.50, then plunged to around 15 cents, which is where it's been for several years.

One of the major problems when investing in penny stocks is that the buy-sell spread, the difference between the buy price and the sell price, can be as high as 90%. If, for example, you buy a penny stock with a 10 cent buy price and a one cent sell price, the stock would have to go up 900% before you could break even. And that's before commission costs are figured in.

While penny stocks are certainly risky, they are really at the bottom of the high risk pyramid. When you start to deal with investments like commodities and options, you really begin to expose your portfolio to risk of serious losses.

Commodities are unprocessed items that can be bought or sold. A market for commodities has been developed to allow buying and selling of such diverse items as sugar, oranges, corn, lumber and pork bellies. Commodities are purchased mainly for speculation and hedging, or protecting against possible loss. Speculators are in the market for only one reason: they expect the price of a commodity to rise or fall over a specific period and so they buy a contract on the commodity. A hedger will use the commodity contract to protect a position that they hold in that commodity. For example, if you are a farmer and you want to protect the price of your corn crop, you can use a commodity contract to lock in a specific price before harvest time.

Those who have the greatest potential for making money in commodities are those with the greatest knowledge of the underlying market. Without this specific market information, the average investor is likely to lose badly. The potential for loss is enhanced by the fact that commodities are purchased using leverage. Leverage means that you are borrowing money to invest.

Options are another high risk investment. An option is an instrument that gives you the right to either buy or sell a security at a specific price for a specific period of time. There are two types of options, calls and puts. A call option is the right to buy a stock in the future at a specified price. A put option is the right to sell a stock in the future at a specified price. As with commodities, people use options to take advantage of where they think a stock will be trading in the future and to protect positions they already have.

Because full explanations of investments in commodities and options are beyond the scope of this book, I have omitted a great deal of information. Suffice it to say that on Wall Street there are professional investors who do nothing but invest in these kinds of securities, and even they admit that consistent success is nearly impossible. Because of that fact, prudent investors should avoid these speculative investments.

Other Danger Areas   As I mentioned previously, prudent investors also avoid leveraging their accounts whenever possible. Again, leverage is borrowing money from your brokerage firm to buy additional securities. For example, fully margined stock accounts allow you to buy twice as much stock as you have invested in your account. With bonds, you can buy up to 10 times as much as you hold in your account. While this may seem like a grand idea when the market is moving in your favor, it can be very dangerous when the opposite happens. As the market moves against your investment, not only can you lose the original amount you invested, you might have to liquidate securities at the lowest point in the market or add more money to the account to keep the account at the minimum required margin level. Don't let market movements make buy or sell decisions for you.

Another investment trap that prudent investors avoid is the concept of making a million over night. This trap appears often in sample copies of questionable market letters that promise spectacular returns. I don't mean for a moment that all investment market letters are bad. I subscribe to several myself. It's just that this industry has exploded in recent years and is relatively unregulated, which frees unscrupulous vendors to make whatever claims they want.

A few years back I asked several of my clients to send to me the market letter offers they received. I was bombarded with hundreds of different newsletters covering every kind of investment imaginable. Stocks, real estate, commodities, market timing, options, technical analysis, gold coins, were all included. Oddly, they all claimed to be the top performing letter. I got a good laugh when I read the performance claims on some of them. "#1 Market Letter when using my unaudited performance figures on the trading day before the full moon."

Okay, I'm exaggerating, but what alarmed me was that they all looked so professional. They were good enough to fool even experienced investors. Be very careful with these market letters. If it sounds too good to be true, it probably is. You should consult a publication called *The Hulbert Financial Digest*[2] to determine the validity of any claims. The Digest is put out by Mark Hulbert who devotes his time to tracking the results of the buy lists of hundreds of market letters.

Another trap to watch out for is telephone solicitation. My clients are constantly bombarded with get rich quick schemes. As a matter of fact, I recently got a call from a client who has about a million dollars invested with me. Someone had called him to offer a way to take a $100,000 investment and increase its value by 50% in only 30 days. It smelled fishy to me, so I called the solicitor.

"We have a bond deal that should net out $38 million by selling $1 billion of Panama bonds to an investor from the middle East," he told me and repeated the claim of turning $100,000 into $150,000 in 30 days. Just to see how far he'd go, I talked him down from requiring a $100,000 investment to where he said he needed only $7,500, and rather than returning $150,000, he was going to give me a million dollars 30 days later. I asked him what the $7,500 would be used for. Legal fees and travel expenses to get to the Middle East, he told me. I ended our conversation, grinning from ear to ear. I don't know about you, but I think the chances of an investor seeing that $7,500 again are about as remote as the $1,000,000 being paid.

What all these examples underscore is the primary concept of prudent investing: longevity. Prudent investors are patient because they want their money to last for the long haul. Benjamin Franklin said, "Money is of a prolific, generating nature. Money can beget money, and its offspring can beget more." If you take high risks, you may be greatly rewarded, but as is far more likely, you will lose money and will have to begin building your portfolio all over again.

**The 5%
Solution**
Some of my clients like to keep a small amount of their portfolio available to invest in high risk investments. I recommend they limit that portion to 5% or less of the risk, or equity component, of their portfolio. The high risk investments I am referring to here do not include commodities and options. The risk of loss is just far too great.

I am referring to things like taking a chance on a hot tip that you read about in a magazine or heard about from your uncle. Clearly, this is a risky proposition because you are buying only one or two stocks — hardly a diversified position. My clients have had mixed results with their high risk money, but they all seem to enjoy taking a chance every once in a while. And I make sure that they only take chances with 5% or less of their money.

What, then, are investments to which a prudent investor should devote at least 95% of his or her portfolio? Quite simply, real estate, stocks, bonds, unit investment trusts, mutual funds and annuities. Because I will be covering strategies for selecting each of these areas in the second part of the book, I will limit this discussion to giving an example of each.

Prudent real estate investors limit real estate investments to those that they can control or to publicly-traded companies. For example, your home is most likely your largest real estate investment and is one that you control. A publicly traded real estate investment would be a real estate investment trust (REIT). A REIT is a company that manages a portfolio of real estate properties. You can buy REITs that invest in things like apartments, manufactured homes, shopping centers, malls, office buildings, health care facilities or hotels. Because REITs trade on the exchanges, they offer liquidity and uniform reporting standards.

Prudent stock investors limit the vast majority of stock investments to exchange-listed stocks. By avoiding penny, unlisted and illiquid stocks, you can reduce some of the risk associated with equity investing. For example, when you buy a company like Coca-Cola, you are buying a New York Stock Exchange listed company that has a more than 15 year record of increasing earnings. Since 1984, this stocks' price has gone from $8 to $65. Buying quality companies that have been improving financially for many years is a good way to reduce the risk associated with equity investing.

Prudent bond investors buy bonds that are issued by the government or highly rated by an outside rating service, such as Moody's or Standard & Poor's. If you limit your bond investments to U.S. government bonds, you will effectively remove all of the credit risk from your portfolio. If you buy corporate or municipal bonds, sticking to those bonds with the highest ratings is a prudent strategy. My bond portfolios are designed to be safe money. If I am going to subject my portfolios to risk, it is going to be in the equity component.

Prudent unit investment trust (UIT) investors buy those trusts that contain stocks or bonds that meet the above specifications. A unit investment trust is simply an unmanaged portfolio of securities. The contents are selected by a professional management organization and usually mature on a certain date. I use UIT's for those clients who have fewer dollars to invest but need to buy a full sector portfolio to provide diversification and keep the volatility in check. For example, a major brokerage firm offers a unit trust that buys a portfolio made up of the top picks of their research departments for the coming year.

Prudent mutual fund investors use these funds for short term cash and equity (stock) positions money market funds, as I said earlier, are the best place to park your rainy day fund. Equity mutual funds are best suited for investors who can't yet afford a portfolio of individual stocks. For people with more money, better options are often available using professional portfolio managers. I'll go into this concept in detail in the second section of the book.

Your income portfolio is probably better off in direct investments — individual bonds, CDs, fixed annuities, closed-end bond funds and UITs. Most income mutual funds have no specific maturity and therefore should be avoided. I believe that you need to know when your income positions are maturing. With maturing positions, you can construct a laddered portfolio, one where there is a bond maturing every year. I will explain in later chapters why a laddered config-uration is so important.

Prudent annuity investors buy annuities only when they have maximized their contributions to other tax-deferred investment plans. Among these would be, IRAs, 401(k)s, Keoghs and 403(b)s. When purchasing annuities, prudent investors consider only those annuities that are issued by highly rated insurance companies. Other major factors when considering annuity purchases are variable vs. fixed contract structures, liquidity features and fees. Your investment advi-sor is well equipped to help you sort out all the considera-tions. Annuities are best suited for those investors who will be 59 1/2 years old soon after purchase or are over 591/2 when the annuity is purchased. The reason is that if you need access to all of the money before you are 591/2, you will be charged a penalty upon withdrawal.

For example, MFS offers a variable annuity contract called the Regatta Gold. Sun Life of Canada (U.S.) issues the con-tract and it is rated AAA by Standard & Poors and A++ by A.M. Best. These are the highest ratings available. The contract offers 13 different portfolios as well as 1, 3 and 5-10 year fixed accounts. In addition, the contract offers a 5% guaranteed annual return until the account doubles, up to age 80. Under the contract, you are allowed to withdraw 10% of contributions on an annual basis. The surrender charge declines to zero based on a 6%, 6%, 5%, 5%, 4%, 4%, 3%, 0% structure. The contract charges are 1.4% and there is a $30 annual contract fee, which is waived if the contract value remains over $75,000 or if the contract is 100% allocated to the fixed account.

Kimberly   Kimberly is a normal, happy, healthy ten-year-old and an only child. She attends elementary school, has friends, lives in a loving home, and has an investment portfolio valued around $75,000. "Lucky girl!" you say. Yes, on the surface she's lucky, but there's more than meets the eye.

She doesn't live with her parents. Her father is in jail and her mother is dead. Her portfolio was created from payments she received as the beneficiary of two life insurance policies on her mother.

What happened to Kimberly is tragic. Her father, a refugee from Communism, married her mother after a brief engagement. Although relatively new to this country, the community accepted him fully and he was in the process of becoming an American citizen. He took all the English language courses he could find, and before Kimberly was born he was working at three jobs. After Kimberly was born, something seemed to snap in his mind. He quit working and became sullen and withdrawn. A couple of incidents caused him to be hospitalized in a psychiatric ward. Within 36 hours of being released from his third hospitalization, he purchased a one-way ticket to Brazil and went home to wait for his wife to return from work. He killed her, hid the body, and disappeared.

Kimberly, then two, was spared only because she stayed with her grandparents while her mother worked. After the murder, Kimberly went to live with her grandparents. However, they realized that they were too old to be much support to her in her teenage years, so Kimberly was adopted by her mother's best friend and her husband.

Her adoptive mother reports, "As guardian, I was given control of the proceeds from her mother's two life insurance policies. I was accountable for over $50,000 of Kimberly's insurance money, besides accounting for the monthly social security payment she will receive until she's 18. I don't believe I can think of a position with much more responsibility." It seems to be a position that requires prudent investing.

Kimberly found security in her adoptive parents, but she needed financial security in her investment portfolio as well. Her adoptive mother wanted her money to be invested prudently because she felt she had no right to put the money in a high risk position. On the other hand, she wanted some growth, too.

We decided on a diversified portfolio of income and equity securities. We put about 50% in an eight-year laddered bond portfolio to make sure that we would have access to maturing money every year and to make sure that the volatility of the portfolio was kept in check. The other 50% we put in an equity portfolio composed equally of value, growth and international stocks. The portfolio has performed well over the last several years, earning about 9% while taking less risk than the S & P 500.

While Kimberly's adoptive mother certainly had the opportunity to invest the money in high risk investments that might have generated a higher rate of return, she chose to be a prudent investor. She realized that avoiding a long shot is the best way to keep the portfolio on the path to long term growth and preservation of capital.

Kimberly's life may be filled with uncertainties as she grows older, but fortunately her portfolio isn't one of them.

The Bottom Line

- Avoid investments that increase your risk without a greater or equal increase in return.
- Limit penny stocks, commodities, leveraged buying, and options to 5% of your equity portfolio.
- If it sounds to good to be true, it probably is.

Chapter 5

Exercises

Indicate whether each is a prudent investment as defined in this chapter. Note that each could be held in the high risk part of your portfolio. Remember, I recommend that you limit your high risk money to 5% of the equity portion of the portfolio. Answers can be found at the end of the exercises.

1. ____ A New York Stock Exchange listed stock with a long term record of earnings gains.

2. ____ Swampland in Florida.

3. ____ Fixed annuity with a 25% to 0% declining surrender penalty over 25 years.

4. ____ Growth mutual fund with solid 10 year performance record that just hired a new portfolio manager.

5. ____ Pork bellies commodity contract.

6. ____ Five year U.S. Treasury note.

7. ____ Phone solicitor offering to double your money in six months.

8. ____ Top performing market letter as measured by *Hulbert Financial Digest*.

9. ____ Poorly rated high-yield bonds.

10. ____ Unit investment trust with a portfolio of penny stocks.

Answers

1. Prudent. While simply investing in New York Stock exchange listed stock does not guarantee success, it will provide for increased liquidity and minimum listing requirements. A long term track record of earnings gains is, in most cases, a very favorable attribute.

2. Not Prudent. From the old expression "If you believe that, I have some swampland in Florida to sell you." While someone may have a legitimate reason for buying such land, prudent investors limit their real estate purchases to more traditional parcels.

3. Prudent investors would run, not walk, away from such a penalty ridden, illiquid contract. Most contracts have a surrender penalty structure that lasts for 7 years and starts at about 7%.

4. Not Prudent. A trick question! While a solid 10 year performance record is definitely a plus, the new manager is not. This fund might still be a good investment, but prudent investors would wait several years for the new manager to prove him/herself.

5. Not Prudent. I recommend that prudent investors avoid commodities unless they have an intimate knowledge of the underlying market. Even then, they are still doing little more than gambling.

6. Prudent. A five year U.S. Treasury note would be a prudent investment for all investors. Its unsurpassed credit quality and liquid secondary market make it a winner.

7. Not Prudent. As stated in the chapter, prudent investors just say no when dealing with phone solicitors.

8. Prudent. Market letters can be an invaluable source of information and investment recommendations. Make sure that any letter you consider has been reviewed by *Hulbert Financial Digest*.

9. Not Prudent. Because high-yield, or junk, bonds often carry lower ratings, they should be avoided in the income portion of the portfolio. These bonds may be used by prudent investors if they are included in the 5% high risk portion of the portfolio.

10. Not Prudent. While a unit investment trust could be a prudent investment, this one is not. The risk of the loss from the penny stock portfolio would make this UIT unappealing.

Footnotes

1 Concept by Peter Lynch, One Up On Wall Street, published in U.S.A by Simon & Schuster, 1989, Published in Penguin Books, 1990, page 267

2 Hulbert Financial Digest — Mark Hulbert, 316 Commerce St., Alexandria, VA 22314, (703) 683-5905

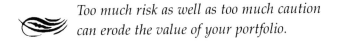 *Too much risk as well as too much caution
can erode the value of your portfolio.*

Chapter Six
The Law of Risk vs. Reward

Risk is one of the hardest investment concepts for anyone to clearly define. Yet clear understanding is essential, because balancing risk against reward ultimately will determine the amount of return that you can expect from your portfolio. This balance is known as the risk-return trade-off. In other words: the greater an investment's potential reward, the greater the risk factor will be.

While seeking an ideal investment, then, a degree of safety is sacrificed for a degree of risk, depending on the tolerance of the individual investor. With that balance and tolerance in mind, I have identified the dream investment.

1. It guarantees a rate of interest at least double the rate of inflation.
2. There is no risk because it's guaranteed by the government.
3. The growth potential is excellent, it will double every five years.
4. You can get out of the investment at any time without penalties or fees.
5. Its earnings are completely tax free.
6. It does the dishes and the windows.

You're right! There is no such investment. In the real world of investing there's no free lunch, no pie in the sky and you still have to do the dishes! You must determine your own risk-return trade off. If you want a high rate of interest from your income investments, you have to give up some safety. If you want growth potential in your equity investments, you have to surrender some income. With every investment, there is a trade off.

To help you determine your risk tolerance, we'll consider various forms of risks associated with investing. There are six basic forms of risk: credit, market, purchasing power, liquidity, interest rate and emotional risk.

1. Credit risk is the risk of principal not being returned to a bondholder because of default by a company or a government. Credit risk is usually greatest in the portfolios of those who chase after high yields. Higher yields are often paid by companies or governments with questionable credit quality.

   The best way to reduce this kind of risk is to learn the rating of any company you're considering for investment. Moody's and Standard & Poor's produce ratings based on an analysis of an issuer's ability to pay interest and repay principal. This is a sample of the bond ratings from Moody's and S&P[1]:

Moody's	S & P	
Aaa	AAA	*High-grade investment bonds.* The highest rating assigned, denoting extremely strong capacity to pay principal and interest. Often called "gilt edge" securities.

| A | A | *Medium-grade investment bonds.* Many favorable investment attributes, but elements may be present which suggest susceptibility to adverse economic changes. |
| Ba | BB | *Speculative issues.* Only moderate protection of principal and interest in varied economic times. (This is one of the ratings carried by junk bonds.) |

Any rating below Baa- or BBB- is generally considered to be junk quality. You'd be surprised how many investors don't know that. I assume that's because in our schools a C denotes average. However, in investing, a rating of Caa or CCC and below denotes a bond in one of the various stages of default.

2. Market risk is the variation in the price of a security caused by external forces not directly related to the performance of the organization that issued the security. These include political and economic conditions, changes in consumer tastes, industry trends, regulatory rulings, and tax preference items. For example, many companies have come and gone over the years as a result of changes in consumer tastes. Fad products have created boom and bust industries that propelled stock prices up quickly and then back down again, sometimes in a period of a few months. As with business risk, you can reduce market risk by investing in those companies that have been around for many years, weathering changes in things like market cycles, tax laws, and industry trends.

3. Inflation risk is a reduction in the purchasing power of the dollar. Inflation can be defined simply as a rise in the

average level of prices for all goods and services. In general, securities, whose values move with general price levels, are most profitable during inflationary times. These include stocks and real estate. Conversely, securities like bonds and preferred stocks that provide a fixed rate of return are negatively affected during periods of inflation.

4. Liquidity, as established in Chapter Three, refers to your ability to convert your investment back to cash. Therefore, liquidity risk relates to the possibility that your investment won't be able to be converted back to cash. A New York Stock Exchange listed stock, for example, has much less liquidity risk than a real estate limited partnership.

5. Interest rate risk is associated with fixed income securities such as bonds and preferred stocks. As general market interest rates increase, the market value of these investments will decrease and vice versa. The longer the maturity of a fixed income investment, the greater the price will fluctuate with changes in interest rates. You can reduce interest rate risk by limiting maturities to around 12 years, or by laddering—varying maturity dates—within your fixed income portfolio. For example, you could buy a portfolio of bonds with five different maturity dates, one year, two years, three years, four years, and five years. Each year, as the bonds mature, you roll the proceeds into bonds with a five year maturity. Bond ladders are very flexible and can be built with many different combinations of securities and maturities.

6. Emotional risk results when you are not certain about or comfortable with your investments and you begin to over-react or under-react to what you hear in the media or from well-intentioned friends and family members.

This can usually be related to the fact that you are not following an investment discipline or that you have not established overall financial goals. You can better manage your emotional risk by following investment strategies that offer exact guidelines for when to buy and sell stocks. For example, you may make a $10,000 investment and decide that at $15,000 you will take your profits, and at $9,300 you will take the loss and look for another opportunity.

These six risks are present to a degree in every portfolio composed of stocks, income securities and cash. In my experience, investors seem to have almost an unlimited tolerance for these risks as long as their portfolios are going up. Unfortunately, portfolios don't just go up, they come down, too. That's volatility. The degree that the six risk factors are present will increase or decrease portfolio volatility.

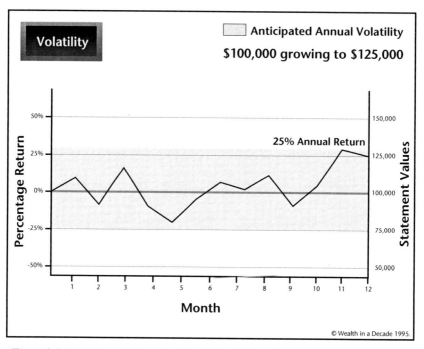

This graph illustrates how much the value of a volatile portfolio can fluctuate over a year while still achieving a 25% return. Many investors cannot stomach that much volatility. The key is understanding the risk associated with your investment style so your emotions don't drive you to make the wrong buy or sell decisions at market highs or lows.

Volatility   Volatility is how much a portfolio goes up and down over time. The greater the volatility, the greater the risk. For example, if your portfolio is made up of highly volatile investments, it can go from $100,000 one month, to $125,000 the next month, down to $75,000 the next month and then back to $100,000. That kind of up and down motion is generally enough to make a prudent investor sick.

Portfolio volatility can mean very different things to different investors. A 20-year-old with 80% of his portfolio in small company stocks shouldn't be surprised if his portfolio goes up or down 30% in any given month. The same volatility to a 80-year-old investor with most of his money in bonds could be devastating financially. You must determine the amount of volatility you can tolerate in your portfolio and then stick to that decision.

I have had clients who said in our initial meeting that they could stand to have their portfolio go down for two or three years during bad market cycles, but who do you suppose I get a call from after about three months of losses? One of two things has happened with these investors. Either they didn't assess their ability to tolerate risk honestly, possibly because they didn't know how, or they had unrealistic expectations about the financial markets. There have been several such cycles, and I can guarantee that there will be several more in the years to come. That's why it's important to assess yourself carefully and honestly.

You need to accept right from the start that the value of your assets will go down as well as up. If you can't accept that fact, you are going to have a lot of sleepless nights and then, because of your anxiety, put your money in investments that don't stay ahead of taxes and inflation. Worse yet, your emotions will cause you to sell your investments when they are down. I've seen it happen again and again during my career. If you learn nothing else from this book, understand well that to stay ahead of taxes and inflation your portfolio must be exposed to some of the six risk factors. With that in mind, it's essential that you assess your risk tolerances, stick to that assessment, and then keep a long-term time perspective with your investments.

Even though there will be some down years, portfolio volatility can be reduced through diversification. Mixing aggressive investments with conservative investments, diversifying between companies and industries, and asset allocation strategies will help you smooth out your returns. Diversification strategies will be covered in much greater detail in later chapters.

Finally, you will actually increase your risk of losing money by playing it too safe. How? If, for example you keep your whole portfolio in CDs, taxes and inflation will be eating away at your returns. The goal is a careful balance between the risk you can tolerate and the reward you need in order to achieve your financial goals within a specified time frame.

What is the effect of taxes and inflation on investments? Let's consider Evelyn's case. She is in the top tax bracket and wants to invest $100,000 in a CD. The bank is offering a 6%, one year CD. This is what her account looks like one year later:

Original Investment	$100,000
One year interest (6%)	$6,000
Total:	$106,000
Minus taxes:	<$2,160>
New Total:	$103,840
Minus inflation:	<$4,102>
Final Total:	$99,738
Net Loss:	<$262>

Even at 6 percent, Evelyn ends up with $376 less in purchasing power, even though her CD paid her $6,000 in interest!

I have seen, with heart-breaking regularity, investors concentrate solely on CDs or short term government bonds. Some are even fully invested in money market. It pains me to see a portfolio invested like this because I know that the investor is probably losing money every day after taxes and inflation. There is a point when some individuals should be 100% invested in income. For example, the portfolios of anyone over 95 years old should be fully invested in income producing securities, however, they should not be fully invested in the money market.

What can you do to find a level of risk that suits you? As a general rule of thumb: One, don't lose sleep worrying about your investments, and, two, when in doubt, always refer to number one. The point is that if you are being kept awake worrying about your money, you're probably invested at a risk level that is too high for you. If your portfolio is 100% invested in money market and you are still losing sleep, I hope for the sake of your portfolio that you just had too much caffeine before bed. The point is that if people are losing sleep while invested in the safest place available, they are doomed to lose money to taxes and inflation.

When determining an acceptable level of risk, you need to consider your spouse or joint investor. Money is one of the leading causes of conflict in marriage, before children that is, and that's just as true when money is placed in risky investments. The best way to prevent this particular conflict is to invest the majority of the money at the risk level of the more conservative person.

John   John is a nice guy. He has principles, is professionally successful, respected and liked by family, friends, co-workers, clients, and neighbors. He describes himself as socially outgoing, professionally aggressive, but reasonable, and generous and caring in relationships. By all accounts, John is a good man.

First as a child, then as a young man, John saw how a lack of money could strain relationships, and he wanted to avoid that. He discovered that for him the key to contentment is to want what you have, not have what you want. "Personal motivation should come from the opportunity to experience and grow, not from having large amounts of money," he says.

When I first met John several years ago, his portfolio was a directionless, contrary mish-mash of investments that appeared to be thrown together. In reality, it was. John called himself a "contrarian," trying to find opportunities in investments that were contrary to the preferences of the general investing public. He said he'd had some luck with "bottom fishing," picking up stocks that were selling at the low end of their yearly trading range. Also, he'd got into some high yield bonds after they fell out of favor, and came down in price, and even dabbled in options and penny stocks.

He admitted that his was a riskier way to invest than prudent investors would consider, but at the time, he wasn't really concerned about losing money. "If I lose, I lose. That's what life is all about. When you gamble, you step up to the window, place your bet and take your chances. If you've evaluated the risks properly, losing money should not be a problem. You should win more than you lose. If you're losing more than you're winning, you just aren't doing a good enough job of evaluating and weighing risk."

At the time, John was 40 years old and his portfolio was valued at about $100,000. Unfortunately, he had taken some big losses from some big bets in penny stocks. Two years after I met him, his portfolio value had been cut nearly in half.

By the time John became my client he was bitter about the whole investment process. Who could blame him? He still had time on his side though; he was only 42 years old and would be earning money for almost another quarter century. "Looking back," he says, "I realize that I used to make some bold statements about gambling with my investments. A couple of bets had paid off and had helped my portfolio grow to $100,000, but I was way off base when I said that you win more than you lose. Obviously, it's the other way around."

When John reviewed his risk tolerance he discovered he wasn't a gambler at heart after all. Penny stocks and options, which had cut his portfolio in half, weren't really a good choice for him. Since he was still relatively young, we both felt comfortable putting him in international stocks and small company stocks, as well as larger value and growth stocks.

It's going to be a slow road taking John back to breaking even from his losses. But he feels that the way his portfolio is invested now is better than careening out of control in a fast car with no brakes.

The Bottom Line:
- Weigh all kinds of risk carefully when planning your investments.
- Realize there has to be some risk to have reward.
- It is possible to lose money being "too safe" because of inflation and taxes.
- Get to know your own risk preference; make a plan with that in mind and stick to it.

EXERCISE

How much risk can you take? Read through the paragraphs that follow and mark the one that best summarizes your feelings. Then mark the one that best summarizes the preferences of your spouse.

1. _____ I never want my portfolio to lose any money. I want access to all of my portfolio all of the time. I realize that I may actually lose money over time due to taxes and inflation.

2. _____ I never want my portfolio to lose any money, but am willing to increase my risk level by buying a high quality, longer term income investment. I know that by holding

the investment until it comes due, I will get all of my principal back. Depending on the maturity and rating of the investment, I realize that I still may lose money due to taxes and inflation.

3. ____ I want to make money with my portfolio, and I am willing to assume the risk of a 10-year bond, realizing that there will be times when my portfolio will be down slightly.

4. ____ I want to make money with my portfolio, and I am willing to have some of my portfolio invested in income investments with longer maturities and large company common stocks (S&P 500). I realize that I am beginning to add diversification to my portfolio. I also realize my portfolio will be down during difficult phases in the investment cycle.

5. ____ I want to make money with my portfolio and I am willing to have some of my portfolio invested in income investments with longer maturities. In addition, I am willing to begin investing small percentages of my portfolio in small company and international stocks as well as larger companies. I realize that I am adding further diversification to my portfolio. I also realize my portfolio will be down during difficult investment cycle phases.

6. ____ I want to make money with my portfolio and am willing to have a fully diversified portfolio with income investments of any maturities and all stocks — value, large company growth, small company, and international. I realize my portfolio will be down during difficult investment cycle phases.

7. ____ I want to invest very aggressively and I am willing to lose a substantial portion of my portfolio if the market goes against me.

Investments to Consider Depending On Your Risk Tolerances

Compare your investment risk with the list below. For example, if your risk tolerance is 4, use the investments listed in 1, 2, 3, and 4. Remember, you may lose money because of taxes and inflation if you chose 1 or 2.

1. Savings accounts, Money Markets, CDs or Fixed-rate Annuities with maturities of a year or less.

2. All the above, plus AAA rated bonds, bond funds or bond UITs laddered to match your need with maturities between two and five years.

3. All the above, plus investment grade bonds, quality preferred stocks, bond funds, target trusts with maturities up to 10 years.

4. All the above, plus value and growth common stocks (large companies), stock funds, variable annuities. Income maturities of up to 15 years.

5. All the above, plus international stocks and bonds and small company stocks. Income maturities up to 20 years.

6. All the above, but add junk bonds and funds, increase percentage of small company and international stock. Income investments of any maturity.

7. All the above, plus a list of options, commodities, other highly leveraged investments, penny stocks. This category, in my opinion, amounts to gambling, and I don't recommend it.

Footnote

1 Fundamentals of Investing, by Lawrence J. Gitman and Michael D. Joehnk, 1990, Harper & Row, page 385

The best way to combat inflation is to invest in common stocks which have a history of outpacing inflation.

Chapter Seven
The Law of Purchasing Power

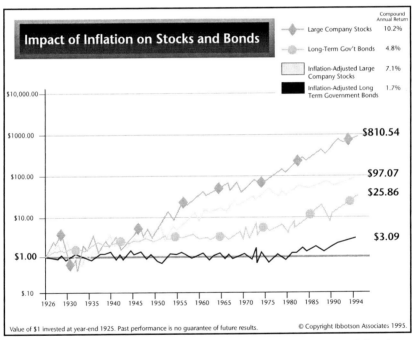

As demonstrated by this graph, the effect of inflation has been quite dramatic over time. Still, stocks have been able to stay ahead of inflation over time and therefore should be included in the portfolio of most investors.

Inflation is inescapable. It's a fact of life. It has been your companion since the day you were born and from all indications it will continue to be with you for the remainder of your life. Will Rogers commented, "Invest in inflation. It's the only thing that's going up." But on the positive side, successful investors know which classes of investments traditionally have beat the heat of inflation.

At any given moment prices are rising for some goods and services and falling for others. That's normal. Inflation occurs when the average level of all prices in the economy rise. Although inflation is watched carefully, moderate inflation is the normal outcome of ordinary economic growth. Although inflation in the United States is relatively low most of the time, there have been periods where inflation has caused some problems. Case in point is the double digit inflation of the late 70s and early 80s. We've had it pretty easy, though. Some developing countries have experienced inflation rates of thousands of percent or higher. That kind of runaway inflation is economically devastating.

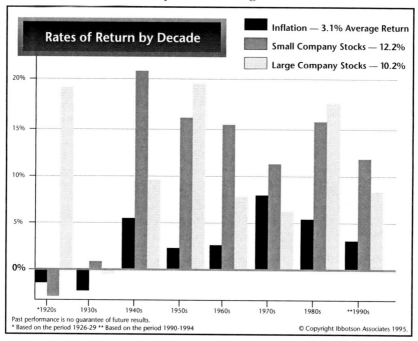

This graph makes a strong case for the importance of long term investing. The 1920s, 1950s and 1980s provided investors with most of their long term returns. On the other hand, the graph illustrates that not every time period will be equally rewarding. The key is to be in the market during periods of truly outstanding performance, not trying to time the market.

Increasing expectations are sometimes confused with inflation. According to Paul Zane Pilzer, author of *Creating Wealth* and consultant to the last three presidential administrations, what appears to be inflation is actually just the population's desire for higher quality and better service.

Pilzer uses an example of a television set. While today's $300 TV is far better than the 1970s $300 model, it no longer satisfies our demand for quality. Therefore, those consumers who happily purchased $300 television sets 25 years ago are not content to continue buying $300 sets today, even though they are getting higher quality at a significantly lower real cost.

Instead of saving money, most consumers today would prefer to spend the same or more in real terms compared to 25 years ago. That is, if they spent the $300 on a TV in 1970, they spend at least $800 today. In return, they end up with a TV that meets the current definition of top quality: a 27 inch screen, high quality stereo sound, picture in picture, and a remote control that can operate other devices like VCR's and cable boxes.[1]

Another example of this is changes in housing expectations. In 1950, the average house size was 1200 square feet. In 1960, the average had increased to 1500 square feet, and by 1980 it had increased again to 2000 square feet. Currently, the average size is 2700 square feet.

It doesn't matter which it is, inflation or increased expectations, the end result is the same: an increase in the average level of prices in the economy. Also, the effect on the economy and markets is the same, and a portfolio must be able to keep up with those effects.

The average annual rate of inflation has been around 3.1% since 1925[2]. Your investments must earn no less than that after taxes just to break even. It's important to consider the long term impact of inflation and whether an investment will ultimately grow to meet your future expenses. Although it's impossible to predict the future rate of inflation, one thing is certain, your dollars will not go as far in five, 10 or 20 years as they do today. If your investments don't keep pace with inflation, your money loses its purchasing power as inflation and the cost of living increase.

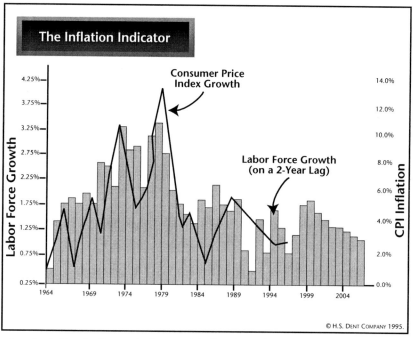

According to Harry Dent's research, the years of the Great Boom Ahead should be characterized by a similar or lower rate of inflation than we are currently experiencing.

When you consider the increasing cost of living, the importance of beating inflation becomes even more significant. The best way to combat inflation is to invest in common stocks, which have a history of outpacing inflation. For example, if you invested in the S&P 500 over an average 10 year holding period, your investments would have outpaced inflation 84% of the time. Over 20 years, stocks would have stayed ahead of inflation 100% of the time[3].

Another example: If you had invested one dollar in stocks at the end of 1925, your investment would be worth $98.37 at the end of 1994, after adjusting for inflation. On the other hand, if you had placed that same dollar in a sock and tucked it under your mattress, it would have only been worth about 12 cents, based on average annual inflation of 3.13%[4].

To further illustrate the corrosive effect of inflation, consider this: IN 1965, on one of his annual trips to Las Vegas, a gambler named Jay won $25,000 after taxes at a casino. Just for reference, Jay could have purchased a modest home for that some of money in 19865. Instead, he put the money in a safe deposit box where it remains today. While the money has been gathering dust, the effect of inflation has made the money worth about $5,000 in today's dollars. If, on the other hand, he had invested the money at 8%, it would have been worth around $80,000—over 15 times as much (assuming a 4% rate of inflation).

The question is not if you can afford to invest in stocks, it is if you can afford not to invest. Stocks are the most accessible, liquid, investor-friendly security that have outpaced inflation over the long haul.

Jeff   Given a choice between working hard, playing your cards right, or being in the right place at the right time, which would you choose as the way to become wealthy? They all work. I know that because each of these adages has been offered by successful people as their reason for wealth.

Jeff is wealthy. How did he do it? He used all three approaches. As a result, he hit the jackpot. When his firm was acquired by another, he received a bonus check for $500,000, and a promotion to a higher paying job in the new firm. Ten years later, his portfolio was valued at over $1.5 million.

Listening to Jeff talk, it becomes apparent that he would have become wealthy even if he had not been in the right place at the right time. Why? Because he had a career plan and an investment strategy. His career plan was to be consistent and take risks where it made sense to take them. His investment strategy is to "buy and hold at least half my portfolio in stocks, the greatest wealth builder out there."

Had you met Jeff back in 1963, when he was overwhelmed with college debts incurred to pay for his law degree, you would not have predicted that he would become wealthy. He was just a young kid with a total net worth of below zero. Hardly a promising start. A further set back appeared to be a philosophy of life that said, "My time is too valuable to spend it on clipping coupons and shopping for bargains." In debt, with no apparent interest in saving money, Jeff was a member of the not-so-exclusive club known as "Financially Floundering."

After a messy and expensive divorce, Jeff decided that the only way he was going to be able to save any money was to force himself into a financial regimen. The best way, as he saw it, was to maximize his contribution to his retirement plan. The money came right out his paycheck so he never had the chance to "forget" to invest. While he had the right idea, he made the all too common mistake of investing in securities that were too conservative. He was invested mostly in Guaranteed Investment Contracts

(GICs), securities issued by insurance companies that guarantee a fixed rate of interest. This investment strategy went on for several years until he saw a report in a financial magazine showing how stocks had traditionally beat bonds in the race to outpace inflation, usually by a large margin. "That report really opened my eyes to the effects of inflation on a portfolio. I vowed right then and there not to let it beat my portfolio."

By maximizing his contributions, Jeff had amassed a sizable balance in his retirement account even before his firm was acquired. Because Jeff still had investable assets even after his retirement plan contributions were maximized, he began working with me to build a portfolio. It's interesting to note that in this investment portfolio, Jeff takes a very low-risk approach. He leaves most of his riskier money in his retirement plan — small company and international stocks make up a disproportionate amount — all in his quest to stay ahead of inflation. Another benefit of keeping most of his equity money in his retirement plan is that the money can grow in a tax deferred environment for maximum benefit.

His other portfolio provides balance. He selects lower risk large company stocks and bonds for his portfolio. His balanced approach to investing has worked. He can lose his job, yet live quite nicely on the over $100,000 income generated by his non-retirement portfolio.

While Jeff is not a typical example, his dedication to trying to stay ahead of inflation by allocating a percentage of his portfolio to stocks is a strategy that should be followed by everyone. You don't need to have 100% of your portfolio in stocks to beat inflation. Far from it. Balanced portfolios can beat inflation as well.

If you would like to ski at Aspen, collect Arabian horses, go yachting around the Keys, or fishing in Canada when you retire, you'll need some money. Staying ahead of inflation is vital if you want to have that kind of money at retirement. When you do retire, and finally get over to the plush spas in Europe, keep your eyes open for Jeff. If he's not there, he will be soon. Introduce yourself, and try to corner him for a minute. It will be a valuable use of your time. You can compare notes and discuss the importance of making sure that your portfolio stays ahead of inflation over time.

The Bottom Line:

- Never make investments without considering the effects of purchasing power over time.
- Common stocks have a strong history of outpacing inflation over time and are a good choice for investors.
- No one's time is so valuable that he/she is unable to hunt for bargains and shop wisely.

Footnotes

1   Television "inflation" example — Creating Wealth, Paul Zane Pilzer, Crown Publishers, Inc., 1990, page 65

2   Ibbotson Associates' CORR Software: Stocks, Bonds, Bills & Inflation and Basic Asset Returns, 1995

3   A Guide to Growth Investing, (actual source: Ibbotson Associates, 1994 yearbook) brochure, Smith Barney research, 1994, page 6

4   A Guide to Growth Investing, (actual source: Ibbotson Associates, 1994 yearbook) brochure, Smith Barney research, 1994, page 7

Chapter Eight
The Law of Monitoring

Successful investors continuously monitor their invest-ments by reviewing the monthly statements they receive from their investment accounts. Instead of fretting over daily ups and downs of the market, they monitor their portfolios, keeping in mind their goals and the time frame for their investments. For example, if you invest in government bonds and plan to hold your bonds until maturity, you have no reason to monitor those investments actively. If, on the other hand, your portfolio is 100% small company stocks, you'd want to inspect it at least monthly.

While monitoring allows you to determine your portfolio's performance, it's vital for two other reasons: accountability and making sure you don't touch your investment capital. First, if you don't monitor your portfolio's performance, you won't be able to determine if your investment selection methods are up to par. Also, you won't know if your finan-cial consultant, portfolio manager, or mutual fund are doing their jobs. If they consistently underperform their peers or the market, it may be in your best interest to reevaluate your relationship with them.

Second, if done properly, the monitoring process lets you determine if you are dipping into your investment capital. Successful investors never touch the capital in their portfolio during the wealth building years. If you need an income from your portfolio, make sure you are spending only the capital gains, dividends and interest that it generates.

Another substantial benefit of monitoring is that it pro-vides an indirect measure of your risk tolerance. One of my elderly clients was invested 100% in an income portfolio by her own choosing. A few years ago, she asked me repeatedly why she shouldn't have some stock in her portfolio. She said that some of her friends owned stock and they were making a lot of money. After several such conversations, I gave in and we bought some stock for her. Her stock position was maybe 10% of her portfolio value and was invested in large, value-oriented companies that I thought would out perform the market.

Beginning the day after she received her confirmations, I got a call from her nearly every day saying that such and such stock was up a half but such and such was down 7/8. That went on for about a month, and then she called and conceded that watching the stocks move up and down was too much for her. Her frequent monitoring showed her that she was too conservative to be in stocks. I sold her out of the stock market that same day. She broke about even after fees and went back to monitoring her income portfolio only when she received her monthly statement.

The primary reason to monitor your portfolio is to see how it is performing, both in comparison to your expectations and to a relevant index, or to the market as a whole. What this means is that if you expect a 12% return from your portfolio and you only got 8% last year, you may have reason to be concerned about its performance — but only if the market was up more than 8%. If the market was up only 7%, your portfolio did its job, but still underperformed your return expectations. That suggests that it may be time to adjust your expectations.

Your expectations for your portfolio will have to be adjusted as time passes and circumstances change. For example, expectations may have to be adjusted if there is a major change in your family, like the birth of a child, or in your financial situation, like getting a new job. Also, shifts in the economy, like rising or falling interest rates, new tax laws, or a broad market correction should trigger a review.

When you don't adjust your expectations in response to these kinds of things, you will become disillusioned with your portfolio and do something that you shouldn't. For example, in late 1994, after constant increases in interest rates by the Federal Reserve that produced one of the worst years for bonds in decades, I was getting many calls from my fixed income investors demanding to know why their portfolios were going down every month.

I explained that as interest rates move up, fixed income prices move down. In fact, they would have lost money if they were invested in something as traditionally "safe" as a two year treasury note. Once I explained this relationship, most of them were soothed and chose to stick it out. In fact, many of them added money to their bond portfolios and actually increased their potential long term returns.

However, I had one client who just couldn't get past the fact that he had lost money, even though almost everyone else in the bond market did too. Over my protests, he had me sell his bonds nearly at the bottom of their fall and put the proceeds in money market. If he'd stuck it out and held them, he would have recouped a lot of the loss, as of this writing in mid-1995, and would still be in great shape holding them to maturity.

Using Market Indices for Portfolio Monitoring

What are the relevant comparative measures for the markets? Over the years, hundreds of averages, indices, composites, and comparators have been introduced. I tend to focus on only five or six of these measures to assess the performance of my portfolios.

The most widely quoted stock market measure is the Dow Jones Industrial Average (DJIA). It's made up of 30 actively traded blue chip stocks that represent approximately 25% of the market value of all New York Stock Exchange (NYSE) stocks, but less than 2% of NYSE issues. Because of the small number of stocks in the average, it is seldom a useful comparative measure. The only place to use this average is in monitoring the value portfolio, as will be explained in the second part of this book.

The Standard and Poor's 500 (S&P 500) is most often used as a general measure for the stock market as a whole. Unlike the DJIA, it is a true index. It relates the price behavior of 500 stocks relative to the base period 1941-1943. It is composed mostly of NYSE-listed companies with some American Stock Exchange (AMEX) and over-the-counter stocks in the following proportions: 400 industrials, 60 transportation and utility companies, and 40 financial issues. This index represents about 75% of the market value of all NYSE-traded issues and 30% of that exchange. I use the S&P 500 to compare the returns of large company, growth-oriented portfolios.

A measure I use to use to track my small company portfolio is the NASDAQ Over-the-Counter Composite. It covers 4500 stocks that are traded over the counter. It represents many small company stocks, but it is also influenced by about 100 of the larger NASDAQ stocks. It is appropriate for my small company portfolio because it often includes a few larger companies.

The performance of international stocks is often tracked with the Morgan Stanley Europe, Australia, Far East (EAFE) index. It covers over 900 securities listed on the stock exchanges of Australia, Austria, Belgium, Denmark, Finland, France, Germany, Hong Kong, Italy, Japan, Netherlands,

New Zealand, Norway, Singapore, Spain, Sweden, Switzerland, and the United Kingdom.

Bond returns are tracked by using one of the Lehman Bond Indices (LBI). Among the indices are those that track most maturities in government, corporate and Treasury bonds, and all the bonds are rated investment grade by the major rating services. All issues have at least one year to maturity and an outstanding value of at least $100 million for U.S. Government issues.

Because in most cases a portfolio will be made up of several classes of assets, you must break down your investments into specific classes in order to monitor them most effectively. My monitoring system breaks each portfolio down into these classes: Cash, Bonds, Tax-free Income Securities, Taxable Income Securities, Value stocks, Large Company Growth stocks, Small Company stocks and International stocks.

You will accomplish two things by breaking your portfolio down into its component pieces. First, you can determine the percentage of total assets that each class makes up. Second, you can compare each class to its relevant index to determine its performance. As you will see in the next chapter, how this data is interpreted is the key to unlocking better portfolio returns.

Determining the percentage total that each asset class makes up is important because it enables you to compare the performance of your portfolio as a whole versus the markets. The performance of your diversified portfolio must be compared to a diversified index for consistency. If you are 100% invested in large company stocks, your task is very easy: compare your portfolio returns to the S & P 500. However, most portfolios contain several asset classes, so you need to consult several indices. When a portfolio made up of bonds and stocks is compared to the S&P 500, investors feel disappointed. But really, they are comparing apples to oranges, and it just doesn't work.

If your portfolio is invested in 60% value stocks and large company growth stocks and 40% bonds, the market you should compare your results to would be 60% S&P 500 index and 40% LBI. If you are invested 100% in stocks, 67% growth and value and 37% international, you would compare your portfolio results to 67% S&P 500 and 37% Morgan Stanley EAFE index. As you can see, simply matching the percentage in each class to its relevant index will give you an appropriate apples to apples comparison.

You have to keep in mind that you need to compare the average life of your bond portfolio to the Lehman Bond Index of a similar maturity. For example, if you have an 8 year laddered bond portfolio, the average maturity would be somewhere between 3.5 and 4 years. You should compare the return of that portfolio to a 4-year Lehman Bond Index, not an 8-year index.

Worksheets   Monitoring is easier if you devise some kind of worksheet to keep track of every investment in your portfolio. It may seem like a lot of work at the time, but believe me, it's much less work than having to dig out confirmations or statements when you need to find out when you bought something or how much you paid for it. Worse yet, most brokerage firms, discounters, and banks do not include date purchased and cost basis information on their monthly statements.

The worksheet should include, at a minimum, the name of the security, the symbol, the date and quantity purchased, the cost basis (what you paid), and the annual dividend or interest payment. For example:

Security Description	Symbol	Quantity	Date Bought	Cost Base	Annual Income
Large Co. Growth Stocks					
Coca-Cola	KO	100	1/2/90	$24	$78
Taxable Income Securities					
U.S. T-Note 7%		10	1/2/95	$1000	$700

You should sit down with your worksheet at least quarterly to figure out the total return of the portfolio. Remember that all dividends and interest must be included in the total return figure. To determine the total return of your portfolio:

1. Subtract the portfolio value at the beginning of the period from the value at the end of the period.
2. Subtract from that amount any money you put into your portfolio or add any withdrawals that you took from your portfolio.
3. Divide the resultant amount by the beginning value of the portfolio. The result is the total return of your portfolio for the period.

For example, assume that Lori's portfolio was worth $100,000 on January 1st. She deposited $12,000 during the year and withdrew $2,000. The portfolio was worth $120,000 on December 31st. To determine the total return of Lori's portfolio.

1. Subtract beginning value from ending value: $120,000 - $100,000 = $20,000.
2. Subtract from that amount ($20,000) any portfolio additions and add any withdrawals: $20,000 - $12,000 + $2,000 = $10,000

3. Divide that number by the beginning value of the portfo-
    lio: $10,000/$100,000 = 10% total return during the year.

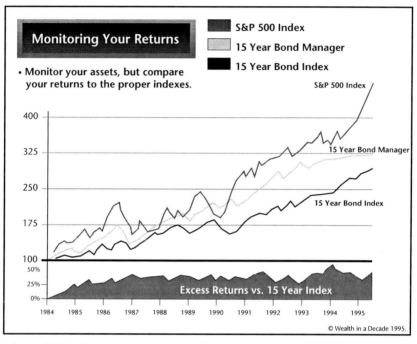

This graph shows the importance of comparing the return of your portfolio to the appropriate index.
In this case, the manager of an actively traded 15 year bond portfolio outperformed the 15 year bond
index. However, if the manager would have compared his returns to that of the S&P 500 index, he or
she would have been quite disappointed. Make sure you are comparing apples to apples.

Depending on your level of sophistication and interest,
you could track many more things on your worksheet, like
Moody's, S&P or Morningstar ratings, analyst opinions, sell
points (both up and down), and dividend pay dates. The
more information you have, the easier it is to make wise
investment decisions.

For investors who are more technically advanced, I recommend putting your investment worksheet on a computer
spreadsheet. Lotus®, for example, makes a spreadsheet that
you can program to compute many investment functions like
gain-loss, total return, average return, and so on. It saves an
enormous amount of time over the old paper, pencil and cal-

culator method. Even better, financially oriented programs like Intuit's Quicken® Deluxe allow you to do much more than monitoring. The program does things like print your checks, pay bills and reconcile your bank statement. It also allows you to keep your home inventory and important records on a single computer disk[1].

While you are doing your quarterly performance review, you should also take some time to make sure that each security is performing as expected. Answer questions like: Has the company increased or decreased its dividend? Is the company still being run by the same management? Are earnings or sales where you projected they would be?

I recommend that husbands and wives, or other joint account holders, work together to monitor their portfolio. Many people enjoy the process of tracking the performance of their portfolios, and it is a good place to introduce uninformed spouses of either gender to the concepts and terminology used in investing. It will also inform them where assets are located. This is useful information for all concerned parties to know in case of illness, divorce or death.

Lou Ann   Lou Ann is a loving mother to her children. She works hard to take care of them and sees no reason to change her ways after 40 years. Although her children are scattered all over the country, she continues to keep in close contact with them. "My children really have been the biggest part of my life. They are good kids, college educated, hard working, and know right from wrong. They don't drink, and they don't do drugs. I think I've done a good job raising them. Looking back, and looking ahead, I have no regrets or worries about my kids. They turned out okay. I wish I could say that about some of the other things that have happened in my life lately."

Perhaps Lou Ann's biggest regret is that while she was a homemaker, she didn't pay close enough attention to financial matters. Of course, it wasn't all her choice. Her husband didn't really want her to know too much about the finances. He had developed a solid career and earned more money each year as he moved up from paint store manager to regional distribution manager for a major paint manufacturer. He was a good provider and told Lou Ann constantly, "Don't worry. If anything happens to me, you'll be well taken care of. In the meantime, you let me worry about where the money comes from."

So Lou Ann didn't worry. She spent what money he gave her for household expenses, house repairs, vacations, travel, clothes, and college for the kids. "I told him what I needed, and he took care of all the financial affairs, controlled the checkbook, monitored the investments, and made whatever decisions needed to be made about money matters. I suppose I should have paid more attention, but I was busy with the kids and the house. Everything seemed to be going okay, and I wasn't really much interested in that stuff anyway. Fortunately, it hasn't turned out to be a problem though, I just talk to Brett whenever I need more money."

Why does she have to call me, her financial advisor? Well, it's a long story. After living together for nearly 40 years, and with the kids gone, Lou Ann and her husband retired. Their future looked secure. They were eligible for social security, had $15,000 in the bank, and a 401(k) plan valued at nearly $400,000.

They made travel plans and started to see the country from the seat of their Honda Goldwing motorcycle. It was something they both wanted to do. "We had the time, so we began to travel."

Unfortunately, less than a year after retirement and before they had completed all their planned trips, they ran out of time. Her husband developed cancer and died in only six months. "The problem with being a farm-raised, unemployed, sheltered wife is that, if anything does happen to your partner, you don't have any idea of what to do. You just naturally gravitate to someone who is supposed to know what's best for you."

After the funeral, one of the toughest tasks facing Lou Ann was figuring out exactly what was in joint ownership and what wasn't. She discovered that all charge accounts were in his name and it was a major problem getting credit. She needed to pay cash for almost everything. It took some legal help to get access to the bank account and the 401(k) monies. Cash was spent quickly, and she had little idea of where it was going. When I spoke with her, about two years after her husband's death, her total portfolio balance had dropped to below $300,000, and was disappearing at a rate exceeding $5,000 per month.

Analysis revealed that Lou Ann, unprepared as she was for this tragic but predictable change in her life, was spending money on things she didn't need. I showed her that at her current spend rate she would be out of money in about four years. In addition, she really had no idea how the portfolio was invested and wasn't tracking the performance of her investments.

She didn't know how. Since all she understood was that her monthly statements showed a declining value, she panicked and began to jump from investment advisor to investment advisor in an attempt to find someone who could stop her portfolio from shrinking. In two years, she changed investment advisors three times. But even worse, as each advisor advocated new investments, she usually ended up selling much of her portfolio and paying commissions, which depleted her reserve even further. What should she do? Whom could she trust? How could she know?

That was when I was introduced to Lou Ann. She told me that she had no experience in investing, hadn't read any books because she didn't know about any, and knew nothing about investments because she'd never had reason to learn. She couldn't answer questions about money saving ideas, concerns when investing, portfolio plans, or conservative actions that could be taken to build portfolio values.

Is her situation typical for women who have spent their adult lives as homemakers and mothers? Yes. In a life filled with the minutiae of home and family, the world of high finance seems, if not irrelevant, at least one detail that can be put aside for the present. In the beginning, Lou Ann's spending was a form of compensation, an effort to deal with the loss of her partner from whom she took her sense of identification. Loss of a spouse can wreak havoc on the bereft partner of either gender. It's just that the woman who earns her living by creating and maintaining a home is very often in the dark financially. It becomes a comfortable, if flawed, arrangement in which the flaw isn't evident until after the death of the wage earner.

The point is, Lou Ann's story isn't attributable to recklessness, but tradition, loss, and a desperate attempt to find her way in a strange environment.

Involvement is a black or white matter: those who have been involved can't imagine it any other way, and vice versa. Most of the widows I've talked with who have been involved with family investments through the years have a hard time believing Lou Ann's story. However, unless both spouses are involved in the couple's financial affairs, the death of one will be a rude introduction to the real world for the uninvolved partner.

I must hasten to note, finance and investing expertise isn't gender determined. There are as many women as men who are very capable at finance and investing, and as many men as women who know nothing about it.

When Lou Ann finally became my client, her portfolio was valued at less than $250,000 and was comprised of a hodge-podge of investments that didn't really serve her. I began by getting her out of most of the high-yield investments that she had been accumulating. I set her up in a laddered portfolio of income securities that would provide her with cash each year from maturing securities. At her annual review, we reevaluate her situation and reinvest the proceeds in the appropriate markets.

After working with Lou Ann for a while I determined that all she lacked was a little instruction. I explained the logic behind the investments I made and helped her set up a monitoring system that made it clear how her portfolio was performing. To help her plug the spending hole, I helped her to set up a budget.

Now she has fun monitoring her investments and she's made it an avocation. She goes to the library and reads reports from Value Line and other sources on the investments in her portfolio. Her heroes are the Beardstown Ladies. She keeps her worksheet current by updating it each time she receives a confirmation from the purchase or sale of any security. We've been able to bring the value of her portfolio back up to nearly $300,000 since we've been working together.

While this may appear to be a happy ending, we've still got a long way to go to get back to where she was five years ago. "After the death of your spouse is the worst time to have to figure out things like investing and monitoring the portfolio. You've got so many other things to deal with. I'd have done it a long time ago if I'd know how important it was. If just one person can learn from my experience, I'll be happy."

The Bottom Line:

- Monitoring allows you to determine your portfolio's performance, provides accountability and helps you to avoid touching your capital.

- Adjust expectations for your portfolio as time passes and circumstances change.

- Don't compare apples to oranges: be sure the monitoring indices you use are specific to each class of assets in your portfolio.

- Joint account holders should monitor their portfolio together.

Footnote

1   Quicken Deluxe — by Intuit, P.O. Box 3014, Menlo Park, CA 94026, (415) 322-0573

How a portfolio is apportioned between stocks, income securities and cash has more impact than market timing or security selection.

Chapter Nine
The Law of Buying Low

Consistently making money over time in the financial markets is possible if you realize that the markets are not gambling casinos, popularity contests, or tests of toughness. They are simply investment arenas. That understood, successful investors know that the best time to buy in a particular sector is when others have lost money in that sector because the prices will be down, usually way down. By the same token, the best time to sell in a particular sector is when the world is still enchanted with that sector. That's the key to making money over time in the "market".

The market I am referring to here is not some general reference to the stock market or the bond market. I'm referring to the same market that you established for your portfolio in the law of monitoring chapter. You can't take on the whole world any more than you can take on or beat the whole market. Focus on where you have your money invested.

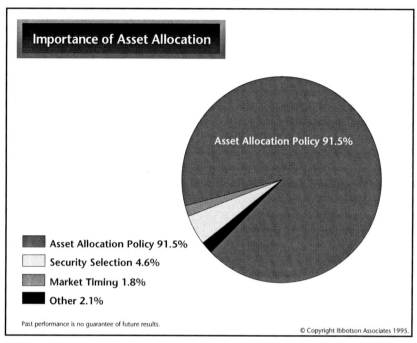

Importance of Asset Allocation

Asset Allocation Policy 91.5%

Asset Allocation Policy 91.5%
Security Selection 4.6%
Market Timing 1.8%
Other 2.1%

Past performance is no guarantee of future results.

© Copyright Ibbotson Associates 1995.

The asset allocation strategy is one of the most important decisions an investor will make. Security selection and market timing are much less important than an overall asset allocation strategy.

Asset Allocation

Where to begin? The answer lies in how you allocate the assets in your portfolio. How a portfolio is distributed between stocks, income securities and cash has a bigger impact on investment return than market timing or security selection. In fact, according to the Financial Analysts Journal, the asset allocation decision accounts for 91.5% of total portfolio return. That may seem hard to believe, but I've seen it borne out over the years. Only about 8.5% is attributable to other factors like security selection and market timing[1].

When I refer to asset allocation, I further break down the general categories of stock, income securities, and cash by expanding the income securities class to include both tax-free income securities and taxable income securities. I also break down the equity class to include small company stocks, value stocks, international stocks, and large company growth stocks.

Asset allocation is important because it provides diversification. Diversified portfolios can iron out a lot of the ups and downs of investing, because not all asset classes go up and down at the same time. The old adage of not putting all your eggs in one basket has considerable merit in assembling a good investment portfolio. Investing your money in only one or a few industries, companies, or maturities can lead to either huge returns or, much more likely, huge losses.

For example, over the years, value stocks and growth stocks have outperformed each other over different intervals. A quick explanation of growth versus value stock investing: Value-stock investors believe that consistent, positive, long-term returns can be achieved by investing in those stocks that are cheap, relative to other stocks in the market. They believe that the market will one day realize the true worth of the company and bid up the price. On the other hand, growth stock investors believe that the price of a company's stock will rise more quickly if that company's earnings grow quickly. They strive to find companies that have excellent prospects for rapid-earnings growth in the future.

There have been four distinct cycles in recent history where growth or value stocks have outperformed each other.

- 1979-80 was dominated by growth stocks.
- 1981-88 was value's cycle.
- 1989-91 was again dominated by growth.
- 1992-94 was another value cycle.

1995 appears to be the beginning of yet another growth cycle. What that demonstrates is that even though the ride was bumpy for both classes, over this time period the performance of value and growth stocks was about the same, and the best way to capitalize on that fact was to have a blend of each in a portfolio. This is just one example of the interrelation between the asset classes. The idea remains the same over all the classes. The end remains the same, too, with a blend of stocks; you end up with a much smoother, risk-adjusted return rate without having to try to time each market[2].

Prior to the 1950s the idea of diversification was still a vague concept. Although investors recognized in a general sense that diversified investment portfolios were beneficial, an explicit technique for crafting a portfolio to meet an investor's particular return and risk criteria didn't exist. That changed after 1952 when an important financial paper by Harry Markowitz presented a framework for quantitatively structuring a diversified portfolio. The paper earned Markowitz a Nobel Prize. By carefully selecting a number of different asset classes, Markowitz showed that investors could achieve desired return with less risk[3].

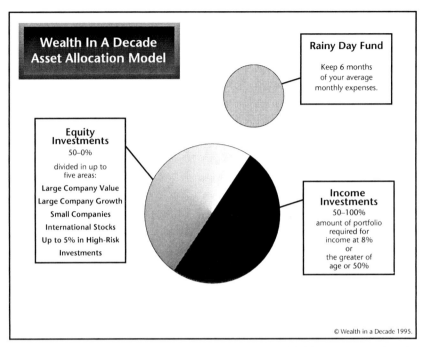

The Wealth In A Decade asset allocation model is a conservative wealth building strategy. It is derived from investors who built their wealth by themselves over the years and is designed to keep your emotions out of your investment decisions. The asset allocation model is based on your age – income investments should make up a percentage equal to your age or 50%, whichever is greater. First, however, you need to make sure your supplemental income needs are provided for by the portfolio. Equity investments make up the remaining percentage and are divided between up to five different classes.

Allocating Your Assets How can you determine the proper asset allocation for your portfolio? First of all, let's define "your portfolio." I'm referring to all of your liquid, investable assets: your brokerage accounts, IRAs, other retirement plans like 401(k)s, etc., should all be included under one blanket asset allocation strategy.

One of the simplest and most conservative strategies is just to subtract your age from 100. Whichever is less, the resulting number or a rule of thumb 50%, is a conservative percentage amount of equity to have in your portfolio. For example, Al is 65 years old. Subtracting 65 from 100 gives 35. Al should have 35% of his portfolio in equity securities. If Jo is 40 years old, she should have 50% in equity. Remember, this is a conservative figure. If you have higher risk tolerances, the amount should be adjusted up or down based on this percentage. The same is true of the percentage you hold in the higher risk equity securities, like international stocks and small company stocks.

Recently an 82-year-old woman who attended one of my seminars moved her assets over to me from another broker who she said had done nothing but lose her hard earned money. Her portfolio was around $400,000, and she knew relatively little about the investment process. I was shocked to discover that her portfolio was comprised of nearly 75% stocks and 25% bond funds. She didn't know why her portfolio was invested like that, nor did she understand the danger of that much stock exposure at her age. Immediately I began to sell her out of her stock positions and put the money in an eight-year fixed income ladder. Gradually, over a period of a few months, I reduced her percentage of equity to about 20%. Today she is much happier with her portfolio.

Here are some examples of the conservative asset allocation decision:

Age	Conservative	Moderate	Aggressive
35	50% Income 17% Value 17% Large Co. Growth 16% Internat'l	50% Income 17% Value 17% Small Co. 16% Internat'l	50% Income 10% Value 20% Small Co. 20% Internat'l
50	50% Income 20% Value 20% Large Co. Growth 10% Internat'l	50% Income 17% Value 17% Small Co. 16% Internat'l	50% Income 12% Value 20% Small Co. 18% Internat'l
75	75% Income 10% Value 10% Large Co. Growth 5% Internat'l	75% Income 15% Value 5% Small Co. 5% Internat'l	75% Income 9% Value 8% Small Co. 8% Internat'l

Once you have implemented your asset allocation strategy, it will need to be adjusted annually. This process is the key to making money over time and one of the most important concepts presented in this book. It is during this crucial annual review that you will uncover your greatest profit-making opportunities. At the same time, don't fight the markets, work with them. You can be like a boxer and sit there and take the punches the market throws, or you can use a martial arts technique of redirecting the opponent's negative energy to your advantage. I've seen many people try stubbornly to buck market trends. Don't do it. You'll lose every time.

Finding Opportunities to Make Money Over Time

How can you find opportunities to make money in the market during your annual asset allocation review? Identify those asset classes that have been under performing and those that have been out performing. It is at this point that the average investor will add money to the hot classes by taking money from the cold classes, thus making the mistake that dooms them to mediocre returns or even losses. I don't condemn them. It's human nature to try to catch a winner and a move that is easily justified. Unfortunately, it's a move that also easily produces sub-par results.

Instead, you need to summon the fortitude to avoid this mistake and pull money from the hot asset class and add it to the cold asset class. When I cover this idea in my seminars, I get about 50 hands waving in front of me.

"Why would I take money out of the class making money?" "Why would I want to add money to the class I've already lost money on?"

Why indeed? Because, by doing so, you ensure that you are following one of the oldest, most quoted pearls of wisdom produced by Wall Street: Buy low, sell high. Although this common sense statement is often said to new investors in jest, it has abundant merit. There have been studies about the disastrous effects of chasing after the hottest market sector or fad. One of my favorites is a study conducted by Lipper Analytical Services. They took all of Morningstar's five-star funds from 1990-1993 and determined what percentage of those funds' performance was below average when compared with the previous year. Morningstar is an independent organization that rates mutual funds and places a lot of significance on past performance. Some of the results of the study showed that in 1991, 71.1% of stock funds and 95.7% of taxable bond funds came in below average. In 1993, 63.6% of stock funds and 55.9% of taxable bond funds posted below average results[4].

How Does It Work   Let's look at an example that will help clarify this asset allocation strategy. Note that the asset classes you see in the example will each be explained in detail in Part II of this book.

When Dorothy was 50 she began the year by using the asset allocation strategy described previously. She needed no income from her portfolio to live on. Her portfolio was allocated with 50% income securities and 50% stocks. Of the stocks, 33% were in value, 33% in small companies, and 33% were international. Her portfolio looked like this:

$300,000	six-year Ladder of Zero Coupon Bonds (50%)
$100,000	Value Stocks
$100,000	Small Company Stocks
$100,000	International Stocks
$600,000	Total Investment

At the end of a year, some sectors had done well and some hadn't. The federal reserve raised interest rates several times.

Congress passed an International Free Trade Agreement with several countries, the President implemented a small business growth package, and women's dress hemlines went up an inch. By popular Wall Street wisdom, the rise in hemlines meant that the stock market would go up. By year end, Dorothy's account value had grown.

$275,000	six-year Ladder of Zero Coupon Bonds
$125,000	Value Stocks
$ 75,000	Small Company Stocks
$200,000	International Stocks
$675,000	Portfolio Value

It's at that point that the average investor executes the big mistake: buy high, sell low. They take money away from the low return sectors (bonds and small company stocks) and add it to the highest returning sectors (Dow stocks and international stocks). However, Dorothy rebalanced her portfolio by applying the advice of Sir John Templeton, one of the most highly regarded global investors: Invest when others are running scared.

Great value often exists when the majority of market participants fear and loathe the market and will sell regardless of price. That's what Dorothy did:

$275,000	Buy $62,500 more Bonds to get 50%	= $337,500
$125,000	Sell $12,500 of Value Stocks	= $112,500
$ 75,000	Buy $37,500 of Small Co. Stocks	= $112,500
$200,000	Sell $87,500 of International Stocks	= $112,500
$675,000	Total Investment	= $675,000

You can see how this method of rebalancing your portfolio is one way of adding to markets that are low and pulling out of markets that may be peaking. And isn't that the whole idea?

Duane   Duane is a type-cast TV doctor of optometry: good looking, age 45, tall, rugged, dedicated, ambitious, and loves a good time. He lives the American Dream: a nice house in the suburbs, two cars, two kids, takes lots of weekend getaway trips, and enjoys flying planes for fun on the weekends.

Duane began his investment portfolio by doing something unusual. He invested in himself. The investment was called "Student Loans." On a balance sheet it wouldn't be called an "asset", it would be a liability. "Starting out with a degree in optometry was critical to my game plan. The problem was, I didn't qualify for much financial aid, and my parents wanted me to make it on my own, so I tried for scholarships and took out loans. The loans made it possible for me to get through school. Of course, the problem then became how to pay them off."

"I was probably more fortunate than some as I was able to earn a salary that allowed me to repay my loans at a rate of $250 per month. The good thing about forcing my budget to cover the loan repayment was that I had to live on less than I made. Once the loan was repaid, I had $250 per month available for investment." By 1982 his student loans were history and his net investment portfolio had one asset. He called that asset "One share of fully paid education valued at unlimited potential."

Being able to earn money on his first job to cover living expenses and pay off his loan taught him how to live within his means. Duane states, "I never did create what I'd call a lifestyle of the rich and famous. I knew I had to repay the loan. So I didn't take on any new responsibilities until I had resolved the ones I had coming out of school. By staying within my talent and ability, I was able to set the stage for the more important things to come, and to prepare myself mentally for the future."

With his loan paid off, he was able to begin a typical investment portfolio. His first step was to open a savings account and deposit $250 per month. When his earnings increased, his deposits increased. As the balance grew, he looked for ways to speed the growth process. His real investment portfolio began in 1982 with a $6,000 deposit into a SEP-IRA account at a major investment firm.

As his portfolio grew, he was having a hard time keeping up with it. It appeared to be out of control as there was no real rhyme or reason to its contents. Sure, it was growing, but Duane figured it was growing more slowly than it should have been. Duane related the situation to his schooling: "The tuition charge with portfolio management is unclear. Unless you really know what you are doing, you may post sub-par results. At least when you go to college, you know what it will cost, and you know that if you do the work, you will be rewarded."

Duane wasn't happy with his broker's lack of direction, so his father suggested he talk with me. I began to overhaul his portfolio to get it positioned where it could take advantage of market values.

"At first I was skeptical, but after a while I could identify each sub-portfolio clearly: large company growth stocks, international stocks, income positions and it made sense. At the end of every year, we sat down together and identified the sectors of the market that had been under-performing and added money to those sectors."

Duane's portfolio has grown to over $500,000 and currently earns about $50,000 per year. He's adding about $15,000 a year. If he doesn't add another penny, and the investments continue to earn 10% per year, he will have a portfolio valued at over $3 million by the time he is 65. That's his payoff for learning to live within his means, to save, and to roll with the market.

The Bottom Line:

- Allocation of assets has a bigger impact than market timing or security selection.
- Diversification will smooth out the ups and downs of investing.

Exercises

Are your investable assets properly diversified, or are all your investments invested in one kind of security? What is your present asset allocation? This should include all of your investable assets: brokerage accounts, IRAs, company retirement plans, etc.

_____%	Cash
_____%	Taxable Income Securities
_____%	Tax-free Income Securities
_____%	Large Company Growth Stocks
_____%	Global Stocks
_____%	Small Company Stocks
_____%	Value Stocks
_____%	High Risk Stuff (hot tips, penny stocks, etc.)
100%	Total Portfolio

What should your asset allocation be?

Footnotes

1 Ibbotson Associates, 1995, from a study entitled "Determinants of Portfolio Performance" by Brinson, Hood and Beebower, published in the July-August 1986 edition of Financial Analysts Journal. Updated by Brinson, Singer and Beebower in the May-June 1991 edition of Financial Analysts Journal.

2 Understanding Value and Growth Investing, Smith Barney Consulting Group, 1993, pages 1 - 2, 5 - 8

3 Investment Diversification Using Asset Allocation, Smith Barney Consulting Group, 1994, page 1

4 "Selling the Future, Concerns About the Misuse of Mutual Fund Ratings", Lipper Analytical Services, Summit, NJ May 16, 1994

*There is one difference between a tax collector
and a taxidermist — the taxidermist leaves the
hide.*

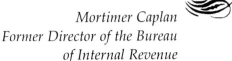

Mortimer Caplan
Former Director of the Bureau
of Internal Revenue

Chapter Ten
The Law of Reducing Taxes ...Legally!

Few subjects anger Americans as fast as taxes, and who can blame us? Our income is taxed at various levels throughout our lives by state and federal governments. Combine those taxes with excise, gas, road, sales and luxury taxes and there's little left over. Finally, there's the estate or "death" tax, which is, in my opinion, the most disgusting of them all. Just when our friends, family and associates are grieving, the federal government is robbing the corpse by taxing our estates up to an amazing 60% if we have accumulated substantial assets during our lifetime.

One of the best ways to accumulate an estate that will one day be large enough to be taxed is by investing as much money as you can in tax deferred vehicles. However, there are various perfectly honorable and legal ways to minimize the bite of taxes. First, we'll look at how to build an estate, then we'll talk about how to protect it.

One of the most overlooked vehicles in all discussions about tax deferral is the common stock. You owe no taxes on the gains of common stocks until they are sold. I have several clients who have held stocks for 30 years or more that have appreciated hundreds or thousands of percent. Some of these stocks have appreciated tens of thousands of dollars. Going one step further, if the owner dies while holding a greatly appreciated stock, the new owner assumes a cost base equal to the price on the date of the original owner's death.

Maximize Your Contributions   The best place to get this kind of tax deferred growth is in programs set up by the government or your employer to help you invest for retirement. These programs, described below, defer the payment of taxes until a specified date in the future when, in most cases, your tax bracket will be lower.

Individual Retirement Account (IRA) is the most basic and most flexible of all self-directed retirement plans to start and maintain. It can be established by any gainfully employed individual who receives income. The Tax Reform Act of 1986 placed limits on the tax deductibility of the maximum annual $2,000 IRA contribution. In order to qualify for a deduction, one of two conditions has to be met: (1) neither spouse can be covered by a company sponsored qualified retirement plan like a 401(k), or (2) adjusted gross income must be below $40,000 on a joint return or $25,000 on a single return. Partial deductions are allowed until incomes go over $50,000 joint and $35,000 single. You can still make contributions to an IRA to take advantage of the tax-deferral even if you cannot make deductible contributions. You can begin withdrawing funds from your IRA at age 59 1/2 and you must start making withdrawals by age 70 1/2.

Gaining popularity are 401(k) plans because of their attractive features: taxes are not owed on money contributed, several investment options are controlled by the participant, and they include matching employer contributions. In 1995, you are eligible to contribute a maximum of $9,240 to a 401(k) plan. That figure is legislated to increase annually as it is indexed to inflation. Monies in a 401(k) cannot be touched until age 59 1/2. A major exception to this rule is that employees can gain access to these assets in the event of a specific financial hardship. You are also able to take a loan from yourself in some cases. The advantage of this arrangement is that you are paying interest to yourself.

There are many other types of retirement plans that you may be eligible to participate in. Another plan, 403(b) plan, is similar to a 401(k) except it is offered by tax-exempt, not-for-profit organizations, like schools and hospitals. Keogh plans are for employees of unincorporated business or those who are self-employed. Keoghs allow you to contribute far more than you can in an IRA or many other retirement plans. Simplified Employee Pension (SEP) accounts are for employees of companies with 25 or fewer employees. Again, SEPs allow eligible participants to contribute far more than other retirement plans allow.

Regulations about these and other plans are often confusing. However, the main idea remains that you can invest some of your money in ways that are tax deferred. Most of these plans do not allow you to withdraw your assets until age 59 1/2, and some allow deductions from taxable income. Consult your company retirement plan administrator or financial advisor for more detailed information on this topic.

Why are there so many different types of retirement plans? Why all the excitement about tax deferred investing? The biggest advantage is triple compounding: You earn interest on your principal, you earn interest on your interest, and you earn interest on the money you would have paid in taxes to Uncle Sam. Clearly, it makes sense to maximize your retirement contribution before you begin any other investment program.

The graph below shows the differences between pre-tax and post-tax growth. It is intended only to illustrate the advantage of tax-deferral. At 7% interest, you would have 70% more money after 20 years.

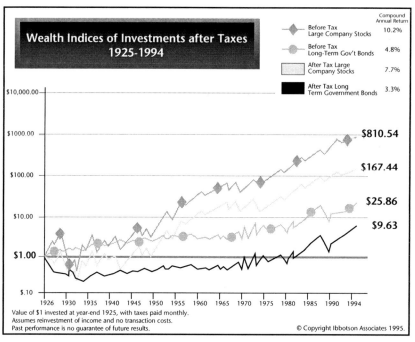

Taxes can take a big bite out of a portfolio's return. This graph makes an impressive case for putting as much money as possible in tax-deferred investments.

   * Taxable results assume no withdrawals and a combined 36% federal and 5% state tax rate.

 ** Tax-deferred results assume no withdrawals. Gains from tax-deferred investments are taxable if withdrawn. If funds are withdrawn prior to age 59 1/2, the IRS will apply a penalty of 10%.

Once you have maximized your contributions to tax-deferred retirement plans, you can explore other avenues of tax-advantaged investing. Annuity contracts are the next best place for some investors to harness the awesome power of tax-deferred investing. These are products offered by insurance companies that offer two main features: Investment earnings are not taxed until withdrawn, and death benefits are provided to a named beneficiary. There are two basic types of annuity contracts: fixed rate and variable rate.

Fixed Rate Annuity Contracts, as the name implies, are guaranteed by the insurance company to pay a fixed rate of interest for a specified period of time. Here are a few ways to get the most from fixed rate annuities:

1. Invest in matched contracts. A matched contract matches the rate guarantee period with the time that you can access your money without any penalties. For example, if you get an annuity that has five years of surrender penalties, make sure the rate quoted is for the entire five year period.

2. Be certain the insurance company is highly rated. There are several rating services like A.M. Best, Moody's, Standard and Poor's, Duff and Phelps, which offer ratings of hundreds of insurance companies. When you put money into a fixed rate annuity, you are literally putting your money into a company's general account. The annuity policy holder usually is insured against loss by the state, but if the carrier runs into financial problems, you might not be able to get to your money for many years. And when you do, you may not have been receiving the stated rate of interest during the period of legal wrangling. Stick with companies with the highest ratings.

3. Make sure you have access to your money. At minimum, a policy holder should be able to withdraw the annual interest without penalty. Better yet, some contracts allow withdrawals up to 10% without penalty.

Variable Annuities are the second kind of annuity contract. These are issued by insurance companies, but instead of offering a fixed rate, you can choose from several investment accounts including stocks, bonds, real estate, gold or international securities. Variable annuities are often described as tax advantaged mutual funds. Here's how to get the most from this type of contract:

1. As with the fixed annuities, stay with quality carriers.
2. Be sure the investment accounts have performed well for a number of years.
3. Be sure the surrender charges end at some point. Most quality contracts have a declining surrender charge that goes down to zero in five to seven years. I've recently seen a contract that had a 12% surrender charge that declined to zero in 12 years.
4. Variable annuities tend to have a number of fees attached to them, like management fees, mortality expenses, and insurance costs. Be sure fees are reasonable, relative to other variable annuities.
5. Be sure you can withdraw at least 10% per year without penalties.

Tax Exempt Securities   Tax exempt securities are an area that may benefit investors in higher tax brackets. One of the most popular forms of tax-exempt investment is the municipal bond. Municipal bonds are debt obligations issued by state or local governments to either finance their general obligations or to finance specific public interest projects like schools, highways, and hospitals. The income generated by municipal bonds is currently exempt from federal income taxes. Also, municipal bonds are generally free from state and local taxes in the state where they are issued. However, there are still tax consequences with the capital gains and losses associated with municipal bonds.

There are two main types of municipal bonds: general obligation (GO) and revenue bonds. General obligation bonds are often considered the most secure type of municipal bond, because they are secured by the full faith, credit, and taxing power of the issuing state, municipality, or territory. Revenues raised from the sale of GO bonds are used to finance the municipalities' day-to-day operations. Revenue bonds are issued to finance the construction of specific projects such as airports, sewer systems, turnpikes, bridges and hospitals. Issuers of revenue bonds pledge to pay the revenue from the financed projects to the bondholders[1].

Municipal bonds do not make sense for all investors. If you are in the lower tax brackets, you may be better off in taxable investments. Also, there is a scarce supply of shorter maturity municipal bonds available for purchase, so it's hard to set up an income ladder using municipal bonds.

Estate Planning   First, it's important that you know that estate planning is complex and may require the input of several professionals including an attorney, tax advisor, accountant, and a financial consultant. That said, let's move on to some specific points about estate planning.

Despite the increased emphasis on wealth production today, many investors fail to consider what will happen to the assets they have accumulated when they die. Without proper planning, a large portion of your wealth could be needlessly lost to probate and taxes. Federal estate taxes are assessed on estates valued in excess of $600,000, with graduated tax rates which range from 37% to 55% and in some cases can be as high as 60%. A taxable estate valued at $2 million, for example, would have an estate tax liability of $588,000. This means that approximately 30% of the assets that you have accumulated would go to the IRS.

In addition to taxes, your estate may also be subject to probate — a time consuming, expensive, and very public process of proving the validity of a will. Probate court proceedings can take from six months to five years to complete, while probate fees, which include court charges, executor's, and attorney's fees can take a sizable bite out of your estate. Estimates vary, but a general rule of thumb is 5% of the value of the assets will go toward probate costs.

The starting point in the estate planning process is to inventory your estate. Many people believe that estate taxes affect only the very rich. However, when you add up the value of your home, life insurance, pension plan, IRAs, stocks, and mutual funds, you could already be above the $600,000 threshold and be subject to estate taxes if you died tomorrow.

Once you have inventoried your estate and have a rough estimate of its value, you should be aware of two important tax provisions: the unified credit and the unlimited marital deduction.[2]

Under the current tax law pertaining to unified credit, every individual estate is permitted a gift or estate tax credit of $192,800, which is equivalent to the estate tax liability on an estate valued at $600,000. Applying the credit at death allows you to effectively pass the first $600,000 of assets to your heirs without federal estate tax.

The second tax provision, the unlimited marital deduction, allows you to defer any or all estate taxes by passing an unlimited amount of property to your spouse. At the death of the surviving spouse, however, taxes will be due and payable on the full value of the estate. Since the surviving spouse is only entitled to an individual tax credit, the estate will receive a single exemption on property valued up to $600,000, not a double exemption on assets worth $1,200,000. In some instances, forfeiting your tax credit could result in additional estate taxes.

Establishing a trust can be an effective way to manage your assets during your lifetime and efficiently transfer those assets to your beneficiaries. It can also help to avoid probate.

A trust is an agreement that you set up with your lawyer under which an individual you select, known as the trustee, holds property for your beneficiaries. You dictate the terms of the trust, and the trustee is responsible for carrying out your instructions. The trust is funded by transferring the title of all or a portion of your assets to the trust name. If the trust is revocable, you retain control of the assets and can change the terms of the trust at any time. If it is not revocable, you give up all rights to the property and cannot amend the trust terms.

There are many types of trusts, each with its own distinct set of features and benefits. For example, the most commonly used trust arrangement, a living trust, is a revocable trust which is created and funded while you are alive. Under this arrangement you can maintain complete control over the trust property, receive income from the trust, transfer property to your heirs, avoid probate, and reduce estate settlement expenses. But, it does not typically provide estate tax savings.

On the other hand, the credit shelter trust provides fewer lifetime benefits but can significantly reduce your estate tax liability. Its purpose is to produce estate tax savings of approximately $200,000 - $400,000 for a married couple. This type of trust arrangement is funded at the death of the first spouse. It will assure that both spouses utilize their unified credit and permits the surviving spouse to manage the investments of trust assets and receive income from the trust. It also avoids probate and reduces estate settlement expenses.

Another common trust is the irrevocable life insurance trust. Its purpose is to remove life insurance proceeds from your estate and avoid estate taxes. This arrangement requires a third party trustee and prevents life insurance proceeds from being valued in your estate. It also avoids probate and reduces estate settlement expenses[3].

Other estate planning strategies include planned giving programs and generation skipping. A planned giving program allows you to give as much as $10,000 annually to any one person without incurring a gift tax liability. A married couple can give an aggregate gift of $20,000 per individual annually. The rationale behind a planned gifting program is to reduce your estate while you are living and benefit your heirs while they might have greater use for the money.

Generation skipping preserves your family's wealth by limiting the number of times that your estate is subject to taxes. By making transfers directly to grandchildren or great grandchildren, your assets will grow and compound tax will be deferred for a longer period of time without being subject to estate taxes. However, if your transfers exceed $1,000,000, you may be subject to the Generation Skipping Transfers Tax.[4]

Again, you should consult your estate planning team to help you determine which strategies are best for you. Contrary to the old saying, what you don't know can severely hurt you, especially when dealing with the complexities of estate planning.

Anton   If you want to know the score of last night's Minnesota Twins game, ask Anton. He knows. In fact, if you want to know anything about the Twins, ask Anton. He's fanatic about baseball, and his specialty is the home town team. He can pull all the facts and figures about the Twins from his head. "I wish I could do the same thing with my investments," Anton states.

The investment game, Anton has concluded, is like the Twins: If you want to get on a winning streak, you have to consistently stay ahead of your opponents. In the investment game, taxes are your opponent.

So who is Anton? Besides being a devout baseball fan, Anton is a father, a widower, and a lifetime prudent investor. Anton describes himself as Mr. Nice Guy. He says, "I'm pleasant, personable, outgoing, and friendly." Ask his friends about Anton, and they'll tell you the same thing.

But Anton is more than just another nice guy. He's a worrier and takes life seriously. Although, when he's stretched up to his full height, Anton's only 5'1", he appears taller because he always wears a hat. Anton doesn't wear the hat because he's hiding a bald spot. "I wear a hat because it makes me look good."

The reason he takes pride in his appearance is because Anton started his working career as a salesman. He learned the importance of appearance early in his professional career. "If you didn't look good, people were less likely to see you. A good appearance is critical to success in life. It helps you to get through the door so you can build a winning record."

"When I started out, money was a problem. As my family grew, money was a problem. Now that I'm close to the end of the line, I don't want money to be a problem anymore." After years of sacrificing and saving, his portfolio is the last thing he has to worry about.

"I respect the value of a buck. That's why after I got married, I said to my wife, 'You can make up the list, but I'll do the shopping.' It's surprising how much a person can save by cutting coupons, watching for bargain prices, and changing tastes to try out the specials that retailers seem to be offering all the time."

His meticulous savings habits rubbed off on his wife as well, and she soon embraced the frugal lifestyle that Anton taught her. Over the years, they accumulated combined portfolios of over $300,000. Then, the unexpected happened. Anton's wife became ill and passed away. Anton suddenly found himself alone after over 30 years of marriage. He struggled with his loss for a long time before he really began to "live" again. Anton decided that life was too short. He wanted time to appreciate the little things and no longer wanted to mess with his investments. He became my client shortly after his wife's death. We were able to roll his wife's IRA into his, thereby keeping the money tax deferred. We also adjusted the cost basis of the stocks in his wife's individual account to the date of her death. She had been holding some of the stocks for many years and the step-up in cost basis on death negated all of the capital gains.

Anton turned out to be a good candidate for annuity contracts as well. While he was still working, none of the companies had any self-funded retirement programs to speak of, so he had to look elsewhere for tax-deferred growth. He already had two fixed rate annuity contracts that he had bought at 9% several years before. We bought three additional annuity contracts — one fixed and two variable — from 3 different insurance companies to decrease the risk. Anton takes full advantage of the withdrawal privileges the annuity contracts offer by withdrawing 10% every year, penalty free. He uses this money and income from some bonds we purchased to provide for some of his expenses. Anton reports, "The bonds were fun because they had more coupons to clip. The annuities were just there and I didn't have to worry about them."

Several years ago we decided that it was time to do some estate planning. We set up a revocable trust with Anton's son as the trustee and sole beneficiary. The trust allows the family to keep complete control of Anton's assets.

Over the years, Anton has developed a portfolio in excess of $600,000. What did the years of saving accomplish? "I'm independent, rent my own place in a retirement complex of other old fogies, and am able to totally support myself financially."

The Bottom Line:

- Have a competent team of professionals on hand to help you plan your estate.
- Maximize contributions to tax-deferred programs like IRA, 401(k), 403(b), Keogh, and SEP.
- Consider annuities after maximizing contributions to your retirement accounts.
- Consider trusts to protect your assets for your heirs.

Footnotes

1   A Guide to Tax-Exempt Fixed-Income Investing, brochure, Smith Barney research, 1994, page 3

2   The Smith Barney Guide to Estate Tax Planning, brochure, Smith Barney research, pages 1 - 2

3   The Business of Life, The Smith Barney Insured Investor Group, brochure, 1994, pages 4 - 5

4   The Smith Barney Guide to Estate Tax Planning, brochure, Smith Barney research, 1994, page 10

PART TWO

How You Can Invest into the Next Century

Introduction to Part II

Congratulations! You made it through the 10 Universal Laws of Creating Wealth. You now have a working knowledge of the fundamental, universal laws which will allow you to begin an investment portfolio, or to better manage the one you already have. Remember that if you violate any of these laws during the wealth accumulation process, you will more than likely be penalized. While you won't be put in jail for the violation, you will certainly pay a fine in the form of lost portfolio growth or income.

This part of the book will show you the strategies I use to manage some of my clients' portfolios. Among my clients are close friends, family, other stock brokers, and people I have worked with for a very long time. They are of all ages. My youngest client is 1 and my oldest is 96. They do many different things. They are homemakers, doctors, farmers, factory workers, lawyers, writers, philanthropists, accountants, and teachers. Many are retired and some are unemployed. In addition, I manage money for churches, schools, American Legion posts, and law firms.

This diverse group represents some of the most different goals, objectives and risk tolerances imaginable. How do I possibly manage all of this money without going insane from the myriad of personal needs and investment products that are available? The answer is quite simple. I only use the following classes of assets for every client I have, myself included: cash, income securities, and equities, that is value stocks, large company growth stocks, small company stocks, and international stocks. These classes are all you need to achieve wealth. That's it. No options. No commodities. No leverage. No penny stocks. No new "Investment of the Day," whatever it might be. Each asset class will be thoroughly explained in a separate chapter.

For the most part I'm not trying to turn you into a financial whiz kid. Far from it. What I try to do in the chapters that follow is to give you an explanation of each asset class as well as the attraction of investing in each class. I also lay out some strategies to use in selecting individual investments for each class, whether through your own research or by using the research of an outside source.

The investment strategy outlined in this part of the book is one that is currently used by many of the wealthy individuals I interviewed while doing background research. As such, it is a relatively conservative strategy. Even when references are made to "aggressive" investors, it is still referring to an aggressive use of this conservative strategy. Why didn't I attempt to lay out moderate or aggressive strategies in this book? First, because many individuals who have accumulated multi-million dollar portfolios have used a strategy similar to the one I developed. They found that while steady growth may not make them wealthy as quickly as other strategies, it does one thing that I believe is critical to investment success: It helps to keep them in the market during periods of poor performance by reducing overall portfolio volatility.

Understanding your risk tolerance and how that relates to extending your time horizon is the one concept that I wish I could get across to each and every person who reads this book. Experience shows me that many investors, especially those who label themselves as aggressive, really have no idea how they will respond if their portfolio loses a great deal of money in the investment markets. I, on the other hand, know how they will respond — they will pull their money out of the market at the very bottom.

This penchant for misunderstood risk and short time horizons is the second reason I only develop this one strategy. Because it is conservative, it will well serve any investor who has not yet been able to determine their actual risk tolerances

— those that only come up after an extended period of negative market returns. It will serve many older, more conservative investors, and it will serve as an excellent starting point for novice investors.

While you are reading through this material, please keep the intent of the strategy in mind. Clearly, this is not the only strategy I use. When I work with investors who have adequately proven their tolerance to risk and demonstrated their long term time horizon, I will gladly offer more aggressive strategies and asset allocations; but I still only need to use the five classes of investments — income securities, value stocks, large company growth stocks, small company stocks, and international stocks.

After you go through these chapters, you will be able to make the decision of whether to implement the strategies laid out in the book by yourself or if you will need help. Remember that a major goal of this book is to present only the information that you need to become wealthy. In meeting that goal, I found it impossible to cover each area to the degree of detail that would benefit all knowledge levels of investor. Therefore, I list other books, seminars, computer programs, and newsletters that may provide additional helpful information.

Before I launch into Part II, let's cover a few points that will aid in your understanding of the material presented.

Mutual Funds   A fundamental concept that you must be familiar with is the difference between a closed-end and open-end mutual fund. But first, a review of mutual funds in general might be helpful. A mutual fund is an investment company that pools the money of many individuals and invests it on their behalf in accordance with predetermined investment objectives. Mutual funds issue shares, each of which represents proportional ownership of all the securities held by the fund.

There are two ways to directly benefit from owning a mutual fund. The first is capital gain, which occurs only when an investment appreciates in value. The second is income, which is generated in the form of interest or dividends.

There are several reasons why investors like mutual funds. One is diversification. Mutual funds generally distribute the pool of shareholder assets across many securities, reducing the potential for any one investment to have a negative effect on the total portfolio. Professional management is another benefit. Few investors have the resources or expertise to analyze securities and companies and to assess trends in the financial markets.

Affordability is yet another reason why mutual funds are attractive investments. The minimum initial investment for most funds is between $250 and $2,500. It would be nearly impossible to assemble a diversified portfolio of individual stocks or bonds for the same amount of money. Finally, many investors like the flexibility offered by funds. They invest in a large "family" of funds and can switch between the different funds in the family often free of charge.

The explosive growth in the fund industry shows investors have responded well to these attributes. There are now over 5,000 mutual funds in existence[1] and several more are being brought to the market on a daily basis. That's more funds than individual stocks traded on the major stock exchanges.

Not only are there thousands of funds, there are also hundreds of classes of funds: growth, growth and income, aggressive growth, small company, capital appreciation, international, global, balanced, flexible, option/income, U.S. Government income, global bond, Ginnie Mae, high-yield bond, national municipal bond, state municipal bond, corporate bond. These are just a few of the classes of mutual funds that are available.

As mentioned previously, there are two types of mutual funds: open-end and closed-end. Open-end funds are the more popular of the two. An open-end fund stands ready to issue and redeem shares of the fund as necessary. Most of the mutual funds that you read about in magazines or hear about in the financial press are open-end funds. Fidelity Magellan, the Janus Fund, Berger 100 and Twentieth Century Ultra are specific examples of open-end funds.

Closed-end funds differ from open-ended in that they offer a fixed number of shares for sale, and they trade on the various stock exchanges. This is one of the primary benefits of the closed-end fund. Open-end fund managers often find themselves buying at very high levels as investors chase a hot market. In addition, they will often have to liquidate the portfolio at bargain levels as investors demand their money back after a bad period in the market. Closed-end fund managers do not have to concern themselves with any money flowing in or out of the portfolio. Instead, they can focus their energies on maximizing return.

I've come to place more and more emphasis on closed-end funds over the years. I like them because they are generally overlooked by the mainstream investing public. Whenever an investment product is overlooked for one reason or another, it creates value. The value in closed-end funds is that it is possible to buy these funds at a market price that is actually lower than the net asset value of what the portfolio is worth. Because price and worth both fluctuate, often independently of each other, the net asset value of the fund can be greater than (premium) or less than (discount) the market value. This relationship can increase return and can increase risk or volatility.

Closed-end funds more often than not trade at a discount to their net asset value. Discounts are created by investor perceptions and supply and demand conditions in the market. Sometimes, discounts can reach levels of 20 - 30%. When these kinds of discounts are around, I am actually buying $1.25 - $1.43 worth of assets for a dollar. That seems like a good deal to me.

For those people who want to do it themselves, open-end funds allow them to make their own decisions and still benefit from professional portfolio management. For those with a small amount of investable assets, I recommend open-end funds because there is no other way a small investor could achieve a safe level of diversification.

After investors have maximized contributions to a retirement plan, they will eventually find themselves with additional money to invest. For those with non-retirement portfolios under $25,000, small investors can use the strategies described in this book to assemble a diversified portfolio made up of income securities, small company, value, large company growth, and international stocks.

Investors with non-retirement portfolios between $25,000 and $50,000 have a few more options, but closed-end funds can still be an important ally for the "do it yourselfer." At this asset level, open-end funds can be combined with closed-end funds and individual bonds and other income securities.

For investors with non-retirement portfolios over $50,000, other investment choices become available. For example, I begin to recommend a managed account structure beginning at the $50,000 level. A managed account uses the services of a professional investment manager, who is compensated on a fee basis. He or she decides when and which investments to buy or sell based on a particular investment objective.

Managed Accounts vs. Mutual Funds   One difference between managed accounts and mutual funds is that the managed account investor does not pool his or her money with the money of other people. Each investor personally owns an investment portfolio consisting of stocks, income securities, and cash that is tailored to his or her unique goals, objectives and risk tolerances. The portfolio manager works on behalf of the managed account investor, not a group of investors, as with a mutual fund.

Another difference involves ownership of investments. Unlike mutual funds, each investment security in a managed account belongs to the investor. By retaining ownership in individual securities, managed account investors maintain a high degree of flexibility and control over the securities. They also retain the voting rights to shares held in their portfolio.

Tax differences also must be addressed when comparing managed accounts and mutual funds. Managed account investors have the ability to make individual decisions concerning securities in their portfolios. At critical times, investors can decide when to hold particular stocks or bonds and when to sell them to realize gains or losses. The ability to select specific portfolio securities for sale enables the investor to implement tax strategies that may not be possible with mutual funds. Funds distribute capital gains to investors at a specified date during the year. If your mutual fund manager sells many securities for gains during the year, it is possible you will have to pay taxes on those capital gains even if you are losing money on your fund investment!

Another difference involves types of accounts that each can be set up in. Certain account types such as Unified Transfer to Minors Accounts (UTMA) generally do not allow managed accounts. Similarly, accounts with check writing privileges often do not permit managed account structures. In each of these examples, mutual funds would be a better option.

A final difference between managed accounts and mutual funds is how cash within the portfolios is managed. Mutual funds must always have a certain amount of cash on hand to pay investors who want to sell their shares. But sometimes, redemptions of a fund will be excessive, and the manager will be forced to sell securities. Managers of individually managed accounts don't face these cash-raising, and sometimes hair-raising, pressures[2].

In review, you will have three ways to implement the strategies presented in this book. You can do it yourself with individual stocks and income securities, you can do it yourself with mutual funds, or you can seek the help of an investment professional to do it for you. Or you can use a combination of any and all of the above. All of these approaches work, and any of them can fail if not executed properly. Keep in mind, if you don't have the time to do a thorough job of researching your investments, consider seeking help.

The Future Is Bright I believe that the future will bring many great things to our lives, and to our pocketbooks. Advances in everything from medicine to computers will revolutionize the way we live. In doing some background research for this book, I came in contact with several economic, technological and quality of life visionaries who have done a great deal of exciting new research about what the future might hold for us. To condense it all, we have two reasons to be excited about the future:

1) The Spending Wave
2) The Technology Wave

The concept of the spending wave was developed by Harry S. Dent, Jr. In his book, *The Great Boom Ahead* and his cassette series "Investment Strategies for the Roaring 2000s," Harry outlines a simple, but historically accurate, method of determining the future direction of the economy. In fact, he projects an 8,500 - 10,000 Dow Jones Industrial Average by 2007.

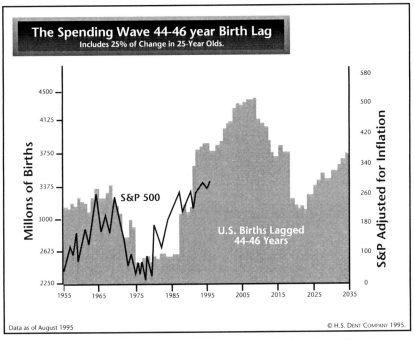

The correlation between the birth rate and the S&P 500 has been quite dramatic over the years. Projecting the data forward, it appears that we truly are in for a Great Boom Ahead.

His research has discovered that the most fundamental aspect of our economy is that it is consumer driven. In fact, about 67% of our Gross National Product comes from consumer spending. Therefore, the best leading indicator of the future direction of our economy is the birth index. The number of births in this country follows an identifiable pattern in that it seems to peak about every 40 years. As everyone is well aware, the baby boom generation was the largest group of births in history. It was so large that it took three waves before it actually peaked in the early 1960s.

Consumer spending begins for most people at around age 19, when the average person enters the work force. There is a surge in durable goods buying around the time people get married at, on average, age 25. Then, after having kids, the greatest buying cycle — cars, homes and furnishings — occurs and peaks at age 46, when on average the kids leave home.

Harry found out that if you project the birth index 46 years into the future for the peak in spending, the resultant chart produces an amazing correlation with the chart for the S&P 500 index up to 1995. However, looking 46 years into the future, the spending of the baby boom generation will peak in the year 2007. The massive rise in spending from now until then will produce the greatest economic boom in our history. Because spending drives corporate earnings, and corporate earnings drive the stock market, Dent projects the Dow to hit the 8,500 - 10,000 level in 2007[3].

The second reason for excitement about the future is the technology wave as explained by Dan Burrus in his book, *Technotrends*. Clearly, the technological changes of the past few years have changed our lives and increased our standard of living. Burrus feels that continued sweeping new technologies will rapidly change the rules that businesses have been operating under for years.

His research has identified 24 technologies that are destined to transform the way companies operate and, as a result, the way we live. Indirectly, these technologies will improve our lives by adding to our investment returns. For example, the relationship between labor and computers will be changing dramatically. Labor costs have historically been rising, while computing costs have been declining. Even as computing costs have been declining, the speed and technology of computers has doubled about every 18 months. While rapid technological advancement like that is frustrating to consumers trying to keep up with current computer products, it will soon allow the average consumer to purchase the equivalent power of a supercomputer for less than $100.

Historically, every time there has been a similar quantum leap in technology, labor resources are freed up to improve the new technology. As a result, the overall standard of living increases. In the example of computers and labor, as more and more production processes become automated by more and more powerful computers, production costs will greatly decrease, leading to a decline in the price of the product being produced. Lower costs lead to improved earnings for the company. Bringing it right down to the individual investor, higher earnings lead to higher stock prices[4].

At the same time that these trends are converging, 90 million baby boomers will be retiring. Because many of these people have done a poor job of preparing for retirement, they will be frantically trying to feather their nest. And where will all of their investment be going? Stocks, bonds, and cash.

Clearly, there is cause to be excited about the growth of the economy as well as the growth of the financial markets. Now is the best time to begin a savings and investment program. Let's get started!

Footnotes

1   Star Tribune, Monday, July 10, 1995, Monday Business section

2   Issues and Answers: Understanding the Differences Between Individually Managed Accounts and No-Load Mutual Fund Investing, brochure, Smith Barney Shearson research, 1993, pages 2 - 5

3   Personal interview with Harry S. Dent, Jr., Fall 1995.

4   Personal interview with Daniel Burrus, Fall 1995.

Chapter Eleven

Income Portfolio

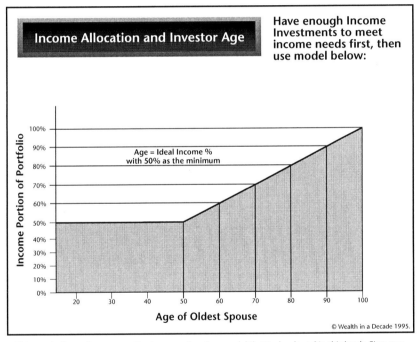

Income Allocation and Investor Age

Have enough Income Investments to meet income needs first, then use model below:

Age = Ideal Income % with 50% as the minimum

Income Portion of Portfolio

Age of Oldest Spouse

© Wealth in a Decade 1995.

This graph shows the conservative income allocation model that is developed in this book. First, you must allocate enough of your income producing investments to provide for your supplemental income needs. Next, you allocate a percentage equal to your age to your income portfolio with 50% as the minimum.

Traditionally, an investor's income portfolio has served three basic functions. One, most fixed income investors used the income produced by their investments to live on. Second, they may have parked their money in fixed income investments because they were safe. Or, third, they reached a certain age where they believed they were "supposed" to invest in fixed income securities.

I am proposing an entirely different use for the income portfolio. It will still form the base from which the rest of the portfolio is built, still provide income to live on, will still be considered "safe" money, and its portfolio percentage will still increase with age. In addition, however, I suggest the income portfolio take on an added responsibility: Providing cash to take advantage of equity investment opportunities that arise at the annual portfolio rebalancing. In that way, your income portfolio will provide you with fresh money every year that will allow you to buy low and sell high in the financial markets.

The correct assembly of the income component is vital to the success of the whole portfolio. The simplest form of asset allocation model dictates that the percentage you invest in your income portfolio should equal your age, or 50%, whichever is greater. If you are 43, you should have 50% in your income portfolio; if you are 50, you should have 50% in your income portfolio; and if you are 80, you should have 80% in your income portfolio.

The only exception to this rule comes into play if you need some of the income produced by the portfolio to live on. For example, assume Bob is retired and needs $12,000 annually to supplement his other income sources. If his portfolio is returning 8%, the first $150,000 of his portfolio must be dedicated to his income needs. If Bob only has $150,000 in his portfolio, 100% will have to be allocated to income investments to provide him with the extra money he needs each month to live on. Remember that because of inflation's effects, I don't recommend that investors below 95 years old be 100% invested in fixed income investments.

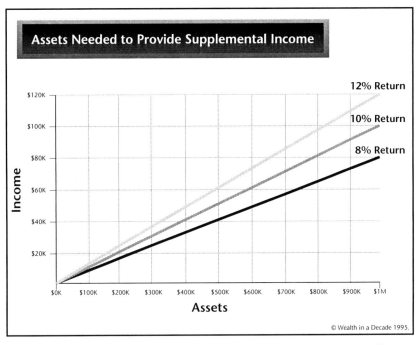

Assets Needed to Provide Supplemental Income

12% Return

10% Return

8% Return

Income

$120K
$100K
$80K
$60K
$40K
$20K

$0K $100K $200K $300K $400K $500K $600K $700K $800K $900K $1M

Assets

© Wealth in a Decade 1995.

This graph illustrates how big your portfolio must be to provide for your income needs at 8%.

Assembling the Income Portfolio
To many investors, the only vehicle used to produce income in a portfolio is the bond. Bonds are definitely a good start, but I take the concept of income one step further. I will use a variety of income producing investments to make up my income portfolios: CDs, fixed-rate annuities, closed-end bond funds, and unit investment trusts. I will invest wherever I can find the best rate of return, while keeping risk at an acceptable level.

Before I explain the various income securities that I utilize in my portfolio, I should say a few words about fixed income investment basics. First, fixed income securities are offered in a variety of maturities ranging from a few days to 30 years and, in some cases, even longer. Generally, those investments with the longer maturities carry greater interest rate risk than those with shorter maturities.

Because of the risk/reward trade-off, longer bonds should pay a higher rate of return. This scenario is the one that governs fixed income securities most of the time and will be the basis for the strategies presented in this chapter.

Another basic concept of the fixed income market relates to bond interest rate sensitivity. When interest rates rise, a bond's price will decline, because its coupon rate is fixed and will be less attractive than the higher rates that will be paid by newly issued bonds. On the other hand, as interest rates decline, the value of an existing bond will generally go up. Remember that if bonds are held to maturity, it does not matter what the prices do in the interim period, because you will get back all of your principal at maturity.

Specific Income Portfolio Investments   While I would consider most any highly rated bond for fixed income portfolios, I tend to focus on U.S. Government bonds. U.S. Government securities set the standard for much of the world's capital markets. They are considered to be the safest form of debt investment, as they are backed by the full faith, credit, and taxing power of the federal government. The government also offers indirectly issued bonds through its federally sponsored or chartered agencies. These issues have the implied backing of the U.S. Government and most experts consider them nearly as safe as directly issued Treasury obligations.

U.S. Treasuries are issued to finance the gaps that occur between the government's receipts and its expenditures. Because there is very little risk of default, U.S. Treasury securities usually pay the lowest rate of interest to investors. However, they are of unparalleled credit quality, and that safety is a large part of what I am looking for in my income portfolios. The types of Treasury obligations include Treasury Bills (T-Bills), Treasury Notes, Treasury Bonds, and Treasury zero coupon bonds.

Treasury Bills (T-Bills) make up the largest component of the money market. T-bills mature in 13 to 52 weeks and are most often used as a short term cash reserve. They are sold at a discount to face value, and the interest earned is the difference between the discounted price and the face value. T-Bills are sold in minimum denominations of $10,000 with $5,000 increments above $10,000. I seldom use T-bills in my portfolios because, for liquidity reasons, I prefer a money market account for short term cash needs.

Treasury Notes have maturities between 2 and 10 years. These are sold in $1,000 minimums. I often use Treasury notes in building bond ladders for clients. They are available in almost any maturity combination and trade on a very active secondary market.

Treasury Bonds have maturities between 10 and 30 years. These bonds also have minimum denominations of $1,000. Because most of my income portfolios are limited to 12 years in maturity, I only use up to 12-year T-bonds.

I also buy a lot of U.S. Treasury zero coupon bonds. Zero coupon bonds pay no periodic interest, and are sold at a deep discount to face value. For example, a zero coupon bond that matures in 12 years may be available for $450. Over 12 years, the bond will work its way from $450 to $1000 at maturity. Zero coupon bonds tend to be more sensitive to changes in interest rates than most other bonds, but that characteristic is nullified by holding the bond to maturity.

Treasury zero coupon bonds are created when brokerage houses buy Treasury bonds and "strip" the interest and principal portions of the bond certificate and sell each separately.

There are many names for these Treasury zeros — STRIPs, TINTs, CATs, TIGRs — but they all were created by essentially the same process.

Compared with Treasuries, U.S. Government Agency bonds often carry a slightly higher rate of interest than Treasuries because of the fact that they are not directly issued by the government. Many government agency bonds are mortgage-backed debt. The majority of mortgage-backed debt is issued by the Government National Mortgage Association (GNMA), Federal National Mortgage Association (FNMA) or the Federal Home Loan Mortgage Corporation. The primary function of these agencies is to increase the availability of mortgage money for residential housing by buying individual mortgages from banks and mortgage companies, then creating mortgage pools that are sold as securities to investors and traded on a secondary market. Investors in mortgage-backed securities do face prepayment risk. This is the chance that homeowners will repay their mortgages before the final stated maturity of the bond. This risk is greatest during periods of declining interest rates as homeowners rush to refinance their older, higher rate mortgages. As a result, mortgage bondholders may find that their investment has been returned to them, depriving them of the higher income stream they had planned on receiving and forcing them to reinvest their money at lower rates of interest[1].

Corporate Bonds, on the other hand are issued by corporations to help build new plants, purchase operating equipment and finance acquisitions. Although my portfolios include only investment grade bonds, I tend to concentrate on bonds that are rated AA or higher by Standard & Poor's or Moody's. These bonds will generally pay a higher rate of interest than comparable U.S. Treasury obligations. They are considered safer than a company's stock because bondholders are creditors and are paid off first in the event of bankruptcy. I never use any junk bonds (those rated below BBB-) in this portfolio, because I am only willing to take risk in the equity component of the portfolio.

Certificates of Deposit (CDs) have been the bread and butter of some of my clients' portfolios for many years. As a result, I will occasionally fit CDs into their ladders. Because I have access to brokered CDs — those bought in bulk by a brokerage firm and resold to brokerage customers — I can often get up to 1% more interest than comparable bank CDs. And, to clear up a common misconception, interest earned on CDs is taxable.

As covered in Chapter 10, fixed-rate annuities are investments issued by insurance companies and pay a stated rate of interest. Maturities are available from 1 to 10 years or more. Interest earned on annuities is also tax-deferred until it is withdrawn. Again, I will fit an annuity into a fixed income ladder if it offers the best rate of return for a certain time period and the individual is near or over 59 1/2 years old.

When using closed-end bond funds, I tend to stick to those that mature on a certain date. These funds are also know as target term trusts. There are many target term trusts that are available to individual investors with maturities out to the year 2009. Most of them invest in U.S. Government Treasury and Agency debt, but some make investments in other forms and ratings of debt. Also, most of them are managed to come due at $10 a share. Recently, some of these trusts which were scheduled to mature in 1996, 1997, and 1998 have declared that, because of the plunge in bond prices in 1994, they will not be able to get the net asset value up to $10 without taking an unacceptable level of risk.

The way to reduce this risk is to only buy these funds at a discount to net asset value. If a fund was to mature at less than $10, you would receive at least the net asset value at maturity, instantly gaining the discount. For example, if a fund was trading at an 8% discount before maturity, you would at least realize an 8.7% gain, plus the dividends that were earned during the holding period. There is one thing that term trust investors must keep in mind: As the trust nears its maturity date, it will have to cut its dividend as the maturity of the bonds in the portfolio gets shorter and shorter.

I began buying some of these target term trusts in late 1994, after one of the worst years in bonds in several decades. For example, in November, I began to buy the Blackrock Target Term Trust, which is scheduled to mature on or shortly before December 31, 2000, at $10 a share. It was trading at about $8 a share and had approximately an 11% discount to net asset value. At the time, it was yielding 8.6%. Because the fund's portfolio is made up of over 50% zero coupon bonds that mature near the fund termination date, it has a good chance of making it back to $10. If it does mature at $10, my clients who purchased at that level will receive $2 per share in capital appreciation (25%) in addition to the annual dividend yield. As previously stated, the dividend may decrease dramatically as the termination date draws near.

Fixed income unit investment trusts (UITs) are similar to bond funds in that they take money from multiple investors and purchase a portfolio of bonds of which each investor owns a proportional part. The main difference is in their management. While bond funds are actively managed, UITs are unmanaged portfolios. This means that unless something goes terribly wrong with the portfolio, it is essentially bought and held until the bonds mature. The trust will not have a single maturity like target term trusts. As bonds mature, the UIT will distribute the par value of the bonds to each investor.

Strategies   One thing that I do require for the majority of my income investments is that they must come due. Each part of the investment must physically mature at an identifiable point in the future. I also require that the income security be purchased with the intent of holding it to maturity. If it is held to maturity, it doesn't really matter how much the market value fluctuates over the years, because it will come due at a specific dollar amount.

The same can't be said for non-maturing income securities. For example, open-end bond funds never mature. You can't be sure that you will get your principal back on a certain day. You don't easily know the average maturity of the fund portfolio. Is it 2 years? 10 years? 28 years? The longer the average maturity of the portfolio, the greater the price may fluctuate. Remember, if the security doesn't mature, you will be subject to the ups and downs of the market if you need to withdraw money.

Because you will need access to money at least annually to capitalize on bottoming markets, you will need to set up your income securities in a "laddered" configuration. A laddered portfolio is set up so that an equal amount of money is coming due every year. For example, if you had $50,000 available to invest in your income portfolio and wanted to go out five years, you would invest $10,000 in securities that come due a year from now, $10,000 in securities that come due two years from now, and so on.

Again, as pointed out in Chapter Eight: The Law of Buying Low, having access to maturing money every year is the key. In the above example, you would have at least $10,000 each year to invest in an underperforming market of your choice. Or, if your portfolio is 100% dedicated to providing you an income to live on, you will be able to roll the maturing money over into new bonds at the top of the ladder.

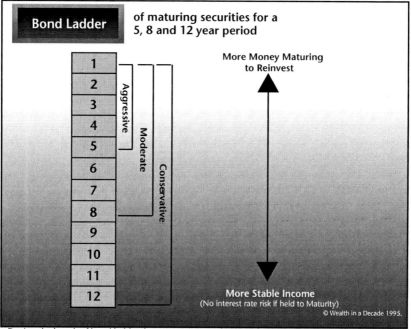

Depicts the length of bond ladder that aggressive, moderate and conservative investors should assemble. More aggressive investors would build a shorter ladder, so they have more money coming due every year. Conservative investors would desire a longer ladder, as it will provide more stable income.

Ladders   How many years should your ladder be? Here is where I tend to move away from "the norm." Conventional wisdom dictates that if you are a conservative investor, you should have a short (5 or 6 year) bond ladder. Conversely, if you are aggressive (keep in mind that this is still a relatively conservative strategy), you should have a longer (8-15 year) ladder. The logic behind this strategy is that bonds have more fluctuation in price as their maturities lengthen. They also should pay more interest.

Therefore, an aggressive investor wouldn't mind seeing his/her portfolio value fluctuate in an 8-15 year ladder if it is earning more interest.

It's at this point that I ask the question, "What does it matter how much the portfolio fluctuates if you hold the bonds until maturity?" Because my income strategy allows you to step into the river of any depressed market, I recommend just the opposite approach. If you feel you are a more aggressive investor (this is still a relatively conservative strategy), build a 5 or 6 year fixed income ladder. If you have a moderate risk level, your ladder should be between 6 and 10 years. Finally, conservative investors should have ladders between 10 and 12 years.

For example, if you feel you are an aggressive investor, a greater percentage of your portfolio will be maturing every year and can be used to capitalize on opportunities in depressed markets. Let's say you have a $150,000 income portfolio, a 5 year ladder, and need no money to live on, then you would have $30,000 maturing every year with which to step into the river of the markets. That's 20% of your portfolio maturing every year. If you built an 8 year ladder, you would have $18,750 coming due annually, or 12.5%. If you had a 10 year ladder, you would only have $15,000 annually, or 10% of the portfolio. Clearly, the shorter the bond ladder, the more you will have available every year to rebalance your portfolio.

An Example   The year is 1999. Assume Tom is 49 years old, considers himself to be an aggressive investor, has a $300,000 portfolio, and he needs no income from his portfolio to live on. Using the asset allocation model, his portfolio is 50% income (50% minimum bond exposure) and 50% equity. His equity investments are divided into one third Value stocks, one third Small Company Stocks, and one third International Stocks.

Tom has constructed a 5 year income ladder that looks like this:

Maturity	Description	Amount	Interest Rate	Interest
2000	CD	$30,000	5.5%	$1,650
2001	Target Term Trust	$30,000	6.25%	$1,875
2002	Treasury Note	$30,000	7.0%	$2,100
2003	Treasury Note	$30,000	7.75%	$2,325
2004	Agency Bond	$30,000	8.5%	$2,550
		$150,000	7.0%	$10,500

His equity portfolio looks like this:

Value	$50,000
Small Company	$50,000
International	$50,000

Assume that a year elapses. Tom turns 50. His portfolio has performed relatively well:

Income Portfolio	Down 5%
Value Portfolio	Up 10%
Small Company Portfolio	Down 20%
International Portfolio	Up 50%

Now his income portfolio looks like this:

2001	Target Term Trust	$28,500	6.25%	$1,875
2002	Treasury Note	$28,500	7.0%	$2,100
2003	Treasury Note	$28,500	7.75%	$2,325
2004	Agency Bond	$28,500	8.5%	$2,550

His equity portfolio looks like this:

Value	$55,000
Small Company	$40,000
International	$75,000

His stock portfolio is worth $170,000, bond portfolio is worth $144,000, he has $30,000 from his CD maturing and he earned about $11,000 in interest and dividends. His total portfolio value is $325,000, a gain of 10% for the year.

Tom buys low and sells high by rebalancing the portfolio as follows: Because he is now 50, he still needs 50% in income ($162,500). As his income portfolio is valued at $114,000, he needs to buy $48,500 in income securities to rebalance that portfolio. After searching each category of fixed income investment, Tom finds an 8.75% Government Agency Bond that matures in 5 years to fill in his ladder. He buys about $33,000 worth ($162,500/5). He also picks up 4 bonds ($4,000) to fill in the other ladder positions — years 2001, 2002, 2003 and 2004. With that the ladder is rebalanced:

2001	Target Term Trust	$32,500	6.25%	$1,875
2002	Treasury Note	$32,500	7.0%	$2,100
2003	Treasury Note	$32,500	7.75%	$2,325
2004	Agency Bond	$32,500	8.5%	$2,550
2005	Agency Bond	$32,500	8.75%	$2,844
		$162,500	7.2%	$11,694

His equity portfolio is rebalanced as follows: ($162,500 / 3 = $54,166).

Value	$55,000	Sell $1000 value stocks
Small Company	$40,000	Buy $14,000 small company stocks
International	$75,000	Sell $21,000 international stocks

There are many scenarios that can unfold with this strategy, and each will be slightly different from the other. For example, it could happen that all asset classes go up during the year. In that case, the one that was up the least would be the best candidate for investment. It could also happen that all asset classes drop during a year. There will still be a class that has dropped the most, and that class will be the best candidate for investment.

The Bottom Line:

- Correct assembly of the income portfolio is vital to the success of this conservative portfolio.
- Income securities should be placed in a laddered configuration to make sure there is money coming due annually.
- Income investments should be held to maturity.
- Aggressive use of this strategy is still relatively conservative.

Footnote

1   A Guide to Taxable Fixed Income Investing, brochure, Smith Barney research, 1994, page 16

Chapter Twelve
Value Stocks

One of the definitions for the word "value" in Webster's New World dictionary is estimated worth. This definition is equally applicable when looking at stock investing. Value stock investors are continually trying to estimate a company's actual or underlying worth. The very base of the value investing philosophy is the belief that the price of a stock doesn't always reflect its true worth. Sometimes, a stock price can be too high; at other times, it can be less than the stock is actually worth. The value investor tries to buy the stock when it is "cheap" and then realize a gain when other investors recognize the stock as underpriced and also begin to buy it.

Value stock investors generally use two different ratios to determine relative value: the price/earnings (P/E) ratio and the price-to-book ratio. The more familiar of the two, the P/E ratio, is calculated by simply dividing the company's price by its current earnings per share. The ratio is then analyzed on an absolute basis in relation to its historical ratios, as well as to similar stocks and the market as a whole. When a stock has a P/E ratio that is less than the average of all stocks traded in the market, or stocks in the same industry group, it is often considered an investment candidate by value investors.

The price-to-book ratio compares the market value of a company with its book value on a per share basis. The book value is a company's total assets minus its total liabilities. Dividing the book value by the total outstanding shares produces a book value per share. Again, when a company has a price-to-book ratio less than the average of all stocks traded in the market, or other stocks in the same industry group, it is considered an investment candidate by the value investor[1].

Unfortunately, proper valuation by using these ratios is becoming more and more difficult as the economy moves from industrialized to service and information oriented. For example, it is much easier to determine how much the assets of a steel company are worth than those of a company that provides consulting services. With the steel company, you simply determine the market value of all of the steel, plant, and equipment. Not exactly an easy task, but it is possible, because all of the items are tangible and can be assigned a value. The consulting company is much more difficult to value, because much of the profitability of the company comes from the ideas and energy of the employees.

How to Outperform the Dow

Despite complexities, there is one unbelievably simple strategy that has been identifying "cheap" stocks, which have significantly outperformed the Dow Jones Industrial Average on a consistent basis for many years. From 1961 through 1992, this strategy has outperformed the Dow 75% of the time. Its average return of approximately 15% was nearly 4% better than the Dow's. In fact, the return was 3% better than that of the S&P 500[2].

Here's the process:

1. Make a list of the 30 stocks that make up the Dow Jones Industrial Average.
2. Determine the dividend yield of each.

3. Put a check beside the stocks with the ten highest yields.
4. Invest approximately equal amounts in these 10 stocks and hold them for a year.
5. At year end, repeat steps 1-4. Sell those stocks that no longer fit in the top 10. Buy those that replace the deleted stocks.

If you do not have the resources to invest in the 10 individual stocks, many major brokerage firms have developed a unit investment trust, based on this strategy. In some cases, you could buy units for as little as $250.

Why in the world does this strategy work? How has it produced such outstanding results over the years? The value indicator associated with this strategy is the dividend yield. A stock's dividend yield is computed by dividing the stock's annual dividend by its price. For example, a stock that pays an annual dividend of $1.00/share, and is trading at $50, has a dividend yield of 2.0%. This relationship between yield and price probably explains why this strategy works in finding value in the market.

If the same stock was trading at $40, the yield would increase to 2.5% ($1.00/$40). At $30, the yield would be 3.3% ($1.00/$30). By selecting the Dow Jones Industrial Average stocks with the highest dividend yields, you are selecting those stocks that are trading at lower prices for whatever reason. These beaten down stocks have a greater tendency to bounce back to their former highs.

One may argue that if the shares are trading at relatively low prices, there must be something wrong with the company. While this is certainly possible, I think that another explanation is more likely. The Dow is made up of a moderately good balance of "cyclical" and "defensive" stocks. A cyclical company is one whose sales, and price, rise and fall with the overall economic or business cycle. Companies of this type include automobile manufacturers, retail stores and construction product makers. A defensive stock is one whose products will be purchased no matter what the economy is doing. In this category are things like drugs, oil, food, or even alcohol and cigarettes. Defensive stocks tend to outperform during economic contractions, precisely the same time that cyclical stocks are lagging.

Because of this phenomenon, if you use this simple strategy, you will generally end up buying those ten companies that are out of favor at that particular time. As a result, you will be in the best position to take advantage of the economic cycle moving from expansion to contraction.

In addition, there is one more reason why I like this method of stock selection. Using this strategy takes emotions out of investing. You can't be swayed by hope, fear, boredom, or greed with this strategy. It creates a discipline that you must follow exactly for you to be successful. Distancing emotions from investments is a goal that all investors should have.

The Dow Jones Industrial Average The stocks that make up the Dow Jones Industrial Average include some of the most widely recognized names in the world. Most readers will be familiar with most of the companies in the Dow Jones Average. Even if you don't recognize the names, there's a good chance that you are using the products, services, or concepts that these companies offer. As a matter of fact, I would bet that as you peruse the list you'll realize that you probably come in contact with a product or service produced by one of these companies several times every day. It's this constant demand that keeps the shares of these companies, and as a result, the Dow Jones Industrial Average, moving ever higher.

Another attractive characteristic of the Dow Stocks is their foreign operations. Many of the Dow companies derive a significant portion of their sales from their foreign sales offices, factories, and distribution centers. The benefit is that you are getting international exposure, while having the risk normally associated with such exposure offset by corresponding domestic operations.

Many investors incorrectly assume that these companies are firmly grounded in the good old U.S.A. To illustrate, I had a client who claimed that he would never invest in foreign markets, because he didn't trust any country but the U.S. As I scanned his portfolio, I discovered that he had large positions in several of the Dow stocks that had significant foreign sales — one had foreign sales of nearly 70% of its total sales. Just to let you know how extensive this is, I've included a current percentage of foreign sales in the descriptions of some of the Dow stocks listed below.

The Dow Stocks[3]

> **AlliedSignal -** AlliedSignal makes aerospace engines and control instrumentation, automotive parts for original equipment markets and engineered materials including chemicals and plastics.

> **Aluminum Company of America (Alcoa) -** Alcoa is the world's largest aluminum company. It has 169 operating locations in 26 countries, and foreign sales account for about 44% of the total.

> **AT&T -** AT&T (formerly American Telephone and Telegraph) was formed as a result of the court-ordered breakup of the Bell System. It is a leading provider of long distance phone services and equipment, and is actively involved in the rapidly-developing global

communications industry. It is also involved in the financial services and leasing industries.

American Express - American Express offers travel and financial services. Principal subsidiaries include American Express Travel Related Services, American Express Financial Advisors and American Express Bank, which provides international banking services.

Bethlehem Steel - Bethlehem Steel is the second largest steel company in the U.S. Its major products include sheet and strip bars, structural shapes, and plates.

Boeing - Boeing is a leading manufacturer of commercial and military aircraft. It produces models 737 through 777 commercial jet planes, as well as helicopters and ground transportation systems. Foreign sales are 54%.

Caterpillar - Caterpillar is the world's largest producer of earth moving equipment and construction machinery. Products include graders, tractors, loaders, compactors, and pipelayers. It also makes diesel and turbine engines and has 29 plants. International business accounts for nearly 50% of sales.

Chevron - Chevron is one of the largest United States-based international oil companies.

Coca-Cola - Coca-Cola is the worlds largest soft drink producer. Major brands are Coca-Cola, Sprite, Fanta and Tab. It also distributes juice products such as Minute Maid, Five Alive and Hi-C. International sales are 67%.

Walt Disney - Disney operates theme parks (Disneyland, CA and Walt Disney World, FL - Magic Kingdom, Epcot and Disney-MGM Studios), makes movies, publishes books, and records music. It licenses its products and sells them via catalog and in its chain of Disney Stores, and it also owns The Disney Channel on cable TV.

DuPont - E.I. DuPont de Nemours is the largest chemical company in the United States. Its chemicals are used in the production of gasoline, nylon, polyester, films, resins, adhesives, electronic products, x-ray products, and pharmaceuticals. Foreign sales amount to 42%.

Eastman Kodak - Eastman Kodak is the world's largest producer of photographic products. Foreign sales amount to about 50%.

Exxon - Exxon is the world's largest publicly owned oil company and has natural gas and petrochemical units.

General Electric - General Electric is one of the largest diversified industrial companies in the world. It produces appliances, aircraft engines, lighting, locomotives, turbine generators and medical systems, and it runs GE Capital Services. Foreign sales amount to 34% of total.

General Motors (GM) - GM is the world's largest automobile manufacturer. It operates plants in 17 foreign countries and derives 22% of sales from off-shore business.

Goodyear Tire & Rubber - Goodyear is the largest tire maker in the world. It produces rubber in 34 plants in the U.S. and 39 plants in 24 foreign countries. Other businesses include chemicals, plastics, and other industrial products. Foreign business accounts for 42% of its sales.

International Business Machines (IBM) - IBM is the world's largest supplier of information processing technology. Its products include mainframe computers, PC's, LAN products, and software. Foreign business is over 50%.

International Paper - International Paper is a leading manufacturer of paper, packaging, and building materials. Foreign sales were 30% of total in 1994.

McDonald's - McDonald's operates, licenses, and services the world's largest fast food restaurant chain. There are now over 15,000 McDonald's in over 80 countries throughout the world. Foreign operations provide about 40% of sales.

Merck - Merck is a leading human and animal pharmaceutical producer. Product names include: Prinivil (treats high blood pressure and angina), Mevacor (a cholesterol lowering agent), Primaxin (an antibiotic), Pepcid (anti-ulcer agent), and Prilosec (for gastrointestinal problems). Foreign sales amount to 29%.

Minnesota Mining & Manufacturing (3M) - 3M is a major diversified manufacturing company. Among its products are recording tapes, adhesives, electrical connectors, medical and dental products, roofing granules, specialty chemicals, cleaning agents, and floor coverings. Foreign sales make up about 50% of total sales.

J.P. Morgan - J.P. Morgan owns Morgan Guaranty Trust Company, which is the fourth largest bank in the United States (based on 12/31/94 assets). Its primary focus is on wholesale banking to large corporations, and it has the largest trust department of all U.S. banks. Approximately 52% of revenues in 1993 came from international operations.

Philip Morris - Philip Morris is the largest U.S. cigarette company. It produces Marlboro, Benson & Hedges, Merit and Virginia Slims cigarettes. The company also makes food and beer products under the following brand names: Post, Jell-O, Kool-Aid, Oscar Mayer, Kraft, Miracle Whip, Velveeta and Miller.

Proctor & Gamble - Proctor & Gamble makes household and personal care items, food, and drinks. Brands include Tide, Cheer, Crest, Ivory, Zest, Coast, Safeguard, Dawn, Joy, Downy, Bounce, Head & Shoulders, Prell, Scope, Secret, Bounty, Charmin, Pampers, Luvs, Crisco, Jif, Folger's, Cover Girl, Old Spice and Hawaiian Punch.

Sears, Roebuck - Sears is the world's third largest retailer. It operates Sears department stores and other stores, including Paint and Hardware, Western Auto and Homelife Furniture.

Texaco - Texaco is one of the largest international oil companies.

Union Carbide - Union Carbide makes petrochemicals, plastics, and specialty chemicals.

United Technologies - United Technologies makes and services aircraft engines. Its Carrier unit makes air conditioners, while its Otis unit manufactures and services elevators. It also includes a flight services division which makes helicopters.

Westinghouse - Westinghouse is a broadly diversified company. Segments include broadcasting, electronic systems, energy systems, environmental systems, and power generation.

Woolworth - Woolworth is the 10th largest U.S.-based retail chain. Major store names (in addition to Woolworth) include Kinney, Foot Locker, Lady Foot Locker, and Champs Sports.

Strategies   Unfortunately, there is no way to replicate the strategy presented above with mutual funds. Therefore, you won't be able to take advantage of it in your 401(k). If your 401(k) or similar retirement plan is your only portfolio, I still recommend that you try to diversify your equity holdings with value stocks. If you have a choice of a fund that operates under a value discipline, allocate a portion of your assets to it. If you are not sure how the fund invests its assets, read the prospectus, which will explain the methods used in selecting stocks. If your retirement plan doesn't offer a value oriented fund, or if you don't feel comfortable trying to identify a value fund, invest in an index fund based on the S&P 500. An index fund attempts to replicate the performance of an index by purchasing those securities that make up the index. Buying an index fund will help to make sure that you are getting returns at least equal to the "market."

The Bottom Line:

- Attempt to outperform the Dow Jones Industrial Average by buying the 10 highest yielding stocks in the average, holding them for a year, and adjusting the portfolio annually.
- If you can't afford to buy the individual stocks, the only alternative to accurately employ this strategy is to buy a unit investment trust offered by some brokerage firms.
- If you want to stick with mutual funds, buy a fund that uses a value oriented strategy.

- If you are not comfortable identifying a value fund, buy an S&P 500 Index fund.
- Compare the performance of the value stock strategy to the Dow Jones Industrial Average.
- Most conservative investors should have no more than 33%, and no less than 20%, of their equity money in value stocks.

Footnotes

1   Understanding Value and Growth Investing, Smith Barney Consulting Group, brochure, page 15, 1993

2   Financial World, "The Dow and Dividends" by Tagannath Dubashi, August 2, 1994.

3   The Value Line Survey, Value Line Publishing Inc., 220 East 42nd Street, New York, NY 10017, (800) 833-0046; Allied Signal, Nov 10, 1995, page 1357; Aluminum Co. of America (Alcoa), May 5, 1995, page 1226; AT&T, April 14, 1995, page 745; American Express, March 10, 1995, page 2149; Bethlehem Steel, May 12, 1995, Page 1409; Boeing, April 7, 1995, page 554; Caterpillar, May 12, 1995, page 1345; Chevron, March 31, 1995, 408; Coca-Cola, May 19, 1995, page 1543; Walt Disney, June 2, 1995, page 1769; DuPont, May 5, 1995, page 1243; Eastman Kodak, March 17, 1995, page 141; Exxon, March 31, 1995, page 411; General Electric, April 28, 1995, page 1009; General Motors, March 17, 1995, page 105; Goodyear Tire & Rubber, March 17, 1995, page 127; International Business Machines, April 28, 1995, page 1096; International Paper, April 21, 1995, page 922; McDonald'sMarch 24, 1995, page 304; Merck, May 5, 1995, page 1269; Minnesota Mining and Manufacturing, June 2, 1995, page 1895; JP Morgan, March 10, 1995, page 2127; Philip Morris, May 19, 1995, page 1582; Proctor & Gamble, April 21, 1995, page 966; Sears, Roebuck, May 26, 1995, page 1662; Texaco, March 31, 1995, page 427; Union Carbide, May 5, 1995, page 1249; United Technologies, May 12, 1995, 1401; Westinghouse, April 28, 1995, page 1020; Woolworth, May 26, 1995, page 1667

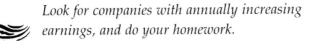

Look for companies with annually increasing earnings, and do your homework.

Chapter Thirteen
Large Company Growth Stocks

Because growth stocks and value stocks go through periods where they out-perform each other over the long haul, you should hold both classes in a diversified equity portfolio. The value stocks, as represented by the ten Dow Jones Industrial Average stocks with the highest dividend yield, are all very large companies. Therefore, I like to balance these large value stocks with large company growth oriented stocks.

Just a few clarifications about the composition of the large company growth portfolio. Sometimes, there will be a few stocks in the portfolio that exhibit value characteristics. These value oriented stocks sometimes end up in the portfolio because of the 10-stock limit that my value strategy imposes. When assembling the large company growth portfolio, I have many more companies from which to choose, and a value oriented company may be an attractive investment candidate. Another thing to keep in mind is that a more mid-sized company may also be included in this portfolio. While there are many different definitions as to what makes a company large or small, the following definitions will be used throughout this book: a large company has a market capitalization (market price multiplied by shared outstanding) of more than 5 billion, while a mid-sized company has a market cap of between 500 million and 5 billion.

Stocks   If you have a long-term investment horizon, one of the most effective ways to increase the value of your portfolio is to invest in common stocks. $1 invested in large company stocks at year end 1925, would have grown to $810.54 by the end of 1994, assuming the reinvestment of dividends and capital gains. If you would have invested the same $1 in long-term government bonds, your investment would have only grown to $25.86, while $1 in T-bills would have only grown to $12.19

Since 1925, common stocks have generated an average annual rate of return of around 10.2% versus 4.8% for government bonds and 3.7% for T-bills. In addition, as I said before, stocks have been one of the only investments that have consistently outpaced inflation over time[1].

How then can you identify stocks that will continue to grow? A portfolio of bad stocks can easily go down, even in a rising market. And it can go down just as rapidly, if not more rapidly, than a good portfolio goes up. That kind of negative price movement is devastating to the long term growth of a portfolio.

I've most often seen losses when portfolios didn't follow some component of the Ten Laws of Investing presented in Part I of this book. For example, I have seen several portfolios that have been improperly diversified. One of the most extreme cases was the investor who had 100% of his stock money invested in one stock. In this particular case, it was a $150,000 position. The troubling thing about it was that it had been an over $175,000 position at the start of the year. This investor had lost 15% of his stock money in less than three months! Even worse, the S&P 500 was up over 5% during the same period.

Large losses in equity portfolios can be caused by one of the   four enemies of proper time perspective: boredom.

Boredom causes people to buy and sell stocks much too quickly and often at inopportune times. I know of an investor who would sell a stock as soon as it went down 5% or more. His definition of boredom was pretty clear cut. Unfortunately, some of the best stocks on the exchanges can trade down more than 5% in one day.

Another mistake that investors make with their equity investments is what I call the hodge-podge portfolio. It usually looks something like this: 100 shares of an off-shore desert research company that a financial magazine swears will go up 50% in the next 3 months; 205 shares of a computer software company bought because of a tip in a market newsletter offer; 500 shares of a computer software company bought because you like the software; and finally, 1000 shares of a computer software penny stock that Uncle Lenny says is a sure thing.

What you end up with is a hodge-podge of companies with no overall direction, no diversification, no mix of stock classes, and usually no hope. In this example, three of the four stocks are computer software companies. The fourth is a company that was probably doomed from the start. This example may seem ridiculous, but you'd be surprised at some of the portfolios I have seen over the last decade. If I ever decide to write humorous books, these portfolios will provide ample material!

Growth Stocks   When doing a fundamental analysis on a company, there are literally hundreds of measures, ratios, figures, and numbers that you can evaluate. Return on equity, debt to equity ratio, unit sales volume, acid test ratio, and profit margins to name just a few. Growth stock investors prefer to keep it simple. While growth stock investors are concerned about some of these items, the main thing they are looking for is earnings. Earnings are what a company has left after costs, expenses, interest, and taxes are taken out of the pot.

Growth investors are looking for annually increasing earnings. Quite simply, they want to be a part of a company that is making more and more money every year. They look for growth in earnings of at least 15%, if not 20%, 25%, or 30%. With earnings, more is usually better. Obviously, growth rates of 30% or more are not sustainable for extended periods of time. When earnings growth begins to slow down, the growth investor is often ready to sell. As you look at charts of many of the greatest growth stocks of all time, their share price moves closely in tandem with their earnings line, both up and down.

What else besides earnings should the average investor be looking for when evaluating large company growth stocks? This question is harder to answer than it seems, because there are literally hundreds, perhaps thousands, of methods of stock selection that have been introduced throughout the years. As with other aspects of my approach to investing, I try to focus on simplicity when picking stocks. Although I use some screens and techniques that are not available to the average investor, I have come across a method that has been quite successful for over eleven years. It is a method shared by the members of the Beardstown, Illinois Business and Professional Women's Investment Club[2]. This investment club, comprised completely of senior women, has become quite a sensation of late.

The club's fairly conservative portfolio has returned 23.4% over the past eleven years including a whopping 53.4% return in 1991. The Beardstown Ladies have developed the video "The Beardstown Ladies Cookin' Up Profits on Wall Street — A Guide to Common Sense Investing" and have written a book entitled *Beardstown Ladies' Common Sense Investment Guide.* Through these items, they have become role models for thousands of new investors. Their information is easy to follow and has produced impressive results.

I met Betty Sinnock, one of the Beardstown Ladies, at a seminar in early 1995. She has recently been given a 3 year appointment to the Individual Investor's Advisory Committee to the Board of Directors of the New York Stock Exchange. I had a chance to interview Betty at the seminar and review the club's strategies for picking solid growth companies that are expected to double in price every 3 to 5 years. It is a method that makes sense from a fundamental analysis standpoint. What follows is just a small part of our interview and can also be found in greater detail in their book and video.

The 9 Factors Betty Sinnock of the Beardstown Ladies Considers When Picking a Stock

1. Industry must be growing and timely. They use the Value Line Investment Survey to determine the top 25 industries. After they have identified industries that interest them, they look at all of the companies in the industry. Value Line makes this easy as companies are grouped by industry, and that simplifies the comparison.

2. Value Line Timeliness rating of 1 or 2. Value Line ranks all stocks for timeliness between 1 and 5, with 1 being the best. Timeliness relates to whether it is a good time to purchase the stock in the opinion of the Value Line analyst.

3. Value Line Safety rating of 1 or 2. Again, Value Line analysts rank stocks for safety between 1 and 5, with 1 being the best.

4. Company debt should be less than 1/3 of total capitalization. If not, find out how the company uses its debt, and if there is a potential for a favorable return to its shareholders.

5. Stock beta between 0.95 and 1.05. A stock's beta is a measure of its volatility, relative to the stock market as a whole. A beta of 1.00 indicates that the stock's price tends to move with the market. A beta of greater than 1.00 is more volatile than the market. A beta of less than 1.00 is less volatile and can be expected to rise and fall more slowly than the market.

6. Projected annual sales and earnings gains of 15% or more over the next five years for small companies, 12-15% for mid-size companies, and 7-10% for large companies. Again, these figures can be obtained from Value Line.

7. Strong management. This is a more subjective measure than the others. It involves finding out the company's plans for expansion, new products, competition, and the like, which could impact the stock price. Betty likes to have the management make the money for her and looks at pre-tax profits to see how well management has been able to curtail costs.

8. P/E ratio at or below 5 year average. The rationale here is that if the stock is trading with the current P/E ratio above its 5 year average, it is probably overpriced and should be avoided for the time being.

9. Price below $25. Because they are an investment club, they have a limited amount of money to invest. They try to stick to stocks trading below $25, because they try to buy even lots of 100 shares, but they will sometimes invest in higher priced shares if they feel it is a good investment.

The best thing about this stock selection method is that it is a system. Without a system, the beginning stock investor will invariably develop a hodge-podge portfolio that will cause nothing but grief. This system does require research but is still easy to follow and implement.

When assembling a portfolio based on this method, you must still follow the 10 Laws of Investing. Make sure you diversify between industry groups, monitor your portfolio and keep a long term perspective. Remember, these stocks are selected to double in 3 to 5 years.

More Pointers   Over the years, I have identified a few other points that all stock investors should remember. First, beware of the low priced stock! A general rule of thumb is that a stock that is trading at a greatly reduced price, independent of the market, is doing so for a reason. The company usually has some major problems with management, its products, the law, or sometimes a combination of all three. Granted, there are a few great bargains at this price level, but "bottom fishing" is usually very tricky. As seasoned garage sale customers have learned, just because something is cheap, doesn't mean its a bargain.

Next, don't equate large companies with conservative stocks. While larger companies are often in the mature phases of their development, their prices can still be rocked by events or regulations that affect the products or services they provide. One of the best examples is what happened to IBM in the early 1990's. For many years, IBM had been considered the bluest of blue chips. Its price had traded as high as $140 in early 1991. After a series of miscues related to its product line, the price plunged to $40 in mid-1993. While the price has since recovered to the $120 level, I think you'd have a hard time finding an IBM stockholder who would say the stock was conservative. According to Peter Lynch, there is no such thing as a conservative stock.

Where To Hold Your Large Company Growth Stocks Because you should be maximizing your contributions to your retirement plan before starting any other investment program, your large company growth stock portfolio needs to begin there. As the number of investment options in 401(k) plans continue to grow, you may be able to select a fund that follows strict growth stock selection methods. Again you should consult the prospectus as to the specific stock selection methods used by the fund.

The growth of the mutual fund industry has made it rather challenging to buy large company growth oriented mutual funds. There are now hundreds of funds devoted to this investment strategy. While most of them will have slightly different stock selection methods, they all should be looking for growth in company earnings and sales.

Selecting a growth fund still needn't be terribly difficult. The first step is to identify all of the large company growth funds out of the 5,000+ funds available today. Many publications, like Morningstar, break down funds into classes to help you in the process.

Once you have identified the universe of large company growth funds, you can weed out those funds other than the top 25 or so based on 10 years of performance. Avoid using 1 year or 3 year performance figures to rank funds. One year is certainly not long enough to establish a record of performance. Three years is better, but still not long enough to determine if a fund's investment objective has just been in vogue for that period. For example, value stock investing may have been the hot sector for a three year period, thereby putting value stock funds at the top of the three year performance charts. Because of the relationship between value stocks and growth stocks, it would probably be about time for growth stocks to take the performance lead.

I also won't buy a fund unless it has had the same portfolio manager for most of the previous five years. In most cases, once the manager leaves, he/she takes along the possibility of future stellar performance. The new manager will often have a slightly different management style, and will have to spend a great deal of time repositioning the portfolio to where he or she is comfortable. In the meantime, performance will usually fall off. If you inspect the ratings, you'll find that most of the top performing funds have had the same portfolio manager or management team for many years.

Once you have narrowed the field of funds down to those with good five year performance numbers and consistency of portfolio management, you should look at a few other variables. The fund should have a low fee structure. Mutual funds charge fees to cover everything from paying the portfolio manager to costs associated with mailing you a prospectus. You should avoid funds that have fees of more than 2%. That 2% is coming out of your return every year. Many funds have fees below 1.5% and certain funds have fees below 1%.

Keep in mind that the fees I am referring to here have nothing to do with the costs to buy or sell the fund. Open end mutual funds are offered under many pricing structures. For example, no load funds charge you nothing to buy shares. With load funds, you are charged a percentage fee every time you make a purchase. Load fund charges average around 4%, but can be as high as 8 1/2%. Make sure you know the sales charges of any funds that you are considering.

You should also consider investing with a strong fund family. A large family of funds will offer you more investment choices. As your fund portfolio grows, you will be able to move money between funds in the family, often without charge. Remember that for tax purposes, the IRS considers transfers within fund families as a purchase and a sale.

You can also purchase large company growth stocks in the form of closed-end mutual funds. Look for the same things that you did when evaluating open end-funds: good long-term track record, consistency of management, and low fee structure. Closed-end funds are not offered in families, however.

Remember that an added benefit of closed-end funds is that you will often be able to buy a portfolio of stocks at a discount to what they are actually worth. Look for discounts that are near their historical high. This is often the best time to invest, because it indicates that both the market and investor perception are at lows.

You can also purchase large company growth stocks in unit investment trusts. Most major brokerage firms offer UITs with portfolios made up of growth stocks.

The Bottom Line:

- If you are going to attempt to pick individual large company growth stocks, make sure you follow a system and that you stick to it.
- If you would like to remain with mutual funds, identify a growth oriented fund with solid 10 year returns and consistency of management.
- You can also purchase unit investment trusts based on growth investment precepts.
- Compare the performance of the large company growth portfolio to the S&P 500.

- Most conservative investors should have no more than 33%, and no less than 20%, of their equity money in large company growth stocks.
- Try to be legally adopted by one of the Beardstown Ladies.

Footnotes

1   Ibbotson Associates, Stocks, Bonds, Bills and Inflation Yearbook, by Roger G. Ibbotson and Rex A. Sinquefield, 1995

2   Interview with Betty Sinnock of the Beardstown Ladies, Fall 1995.

Chapter Fourteen
Small Company Stocks

While it's easy to make a case for investing in large company stocks which have consistently outperformed bonds, cash, and inflation over the years, it's even easier to make a case for small company stocks — those stocks with under $500 million in market capitalization. According to Ibbotson Associates, while large company stocks returned over 10.2% over the last 69 years ending December 31, 1994, small company stocks have returned around 12.2%[1]. What difference does a seemingly paltry 2.0% make? $10,000 invested at 10.2% in 1925 would have grown to over $8.1 million. That same $10,000 invested in small company stocks would have grown to over $28 million.

There have been many people who have made a lot of money in small cap stocks. One of the most outstanding over the last several years has been Lee Kopp, founder of Kopp Investment Advisors of Edina, Minnesota, established in 1990. Kopp's emerging growth account returned 101.7% in 1991, 34.43% in 1992, 58.49% in 1993, and 25.95% in 1994, a very tough year for growth oriented managers. Clearly, these kinds of returns are not sustainable over any extended period of time, but they do show the potential afforded by small company stocks that you couldn't find in any other sector, save perhaps international stocks.

Kopp knows that following an unemotional investment strategy and maintaining a long term time perspective are vitally important when investing. He feels that way especially about small company stocks, almost more so than with any other investment, because small company stocks have the potential to move up, or down, 20% or more in a quarter.

Kopp refuses to work with those clients that are unable to stomach the normal ups and downs of the small company stock market. Why? Because his experience has shown that their emotions will cause them to pull their money out of the market at the worst possible time. To combat this fact, he offers an extensive risk education program to all his clients. In 1990, one of Kopp's aggressive accounts plunged 25% in just one quarter. Because of the risk education program, he didn't lose one client after this loss. Kopp states, "The key is to ride through the down quarters and to be there for the good quarters, because they come along. As certain as anything, they come along."[2]

Even with all the education Kopp offers concerning risk, from time to time he does get a jittery client or two. Kopp reflects, "I remember one client that came to me with just under $400,000. In a little more than three years, he called me and complained about the volatility of his account, which had grown to $1.3 million. He wanted to move half his money to bonds, but because he was getting jittery, I suggested he move all his money to bonds. I don't really know what happened to his portfolio, but if he would have stuck to his strategy, his account would have been worth over $2 million six months later."[3]

What's the Big Deal About Small Companies? Why have shares of small company stocks appreciated so much more than any other domestic investment? The answer is that the price of these stocks is driven up by rapidly growing earnings and sales. The faster the rate of growth the better. For example, if a large company with several products on the market and $750 million in sales were to introduce a new product, it probably wouldn't add that much to sales growth.

On the other hand, that same new product could have a dramatic impact on a company with only $50 million in sales. The product's introduction could drive up the smaller company's earnings by 50% or even 100%. And that's when investors step in to bid up the price of the stock, trying frantically to get on board of this rapid grower. Because this type of growth is impossible to sustain, it is important to identify these companies very early in their development.

Early in their development does not necessarily mean a low-priced stock. Although there are many small company stocks that do trade in the single digits, I usually don't consider them until they are above $10. I will buy special situations if the price is between $5 and $10. I never buy a stock below $5. The main reason is that the big institutions generally don't buy stocks that are below $5. Institutional buying (mutual funds, pensions, etc.) is one of the biggest catalysts of demand that will drive up the price of a small company stock. Once the possibility of institutional ownership is removed, so is much of the hope of price appreciation.

Another characteristic of small company stocks is that they seldom pay a dividend. This is because they are plowing back as much of their earnings as possible into product development, new equipment development, or market research. These expenses are what will fuel the rapid growth in share price. The companies that have grown the fastest over the years are those that spent the money to develop an innovative product in a distinct market niche.

There have been hundreds of examples of this throughout stock market history. Syntex shot up 450% in 6 months in 1963 after the company began marketing oral contraceptives, better known as "The Pill."[4] Another example: between 1962 and 1964, shares of Xerox appreciated 550% after the introduction of the first high quality, ordinary paper copying machine.

Buying Small Company Stocks Because the small company stock market moves extremely quickly, I rely on outside sources of information for my research. Over the years, I've identified the best source of statistics used to determine potential small company stocks winners: Louis Navellier's MPT Review market letter[5]. If an investor would have put $50,000 in one of his model portfolios in October, 1984, it would have grown to $1.7 million dollars as of July, 1995. That's right around a 3,300% gain.

Navellier has dedicated his career to finding and exploiting inefficiencies that exist in the small company stock markets. He developed a proprietary computer program that uses the ideas behind Modern Portfolio Theory (MPT) as developed by William F. Sharpe and Harry Markowitz. The idea behind MPT is to minimize risk while maximizing returns, by analyzing a company's "alpha." Alpha is a figure that represents the amount of return expected from an investment's inherent value, regardless of market trends.

Navellier uses his computer to scan about 6,000 stocks each week. By crunching alpha's and standard deviations, his computer ranks the top 6% in order of risk versus reward. These stocks make up the "buy list" in his MPT Review market letter. After this computer selection, he applies further screens based on the following fundamental characteristics:

1. Excellent earnings growth, both historically and as projected by Wall Street analysts.
2. A history of profit margin expansion and increasing sales.

3. A record of positive earnings surprises.

It is the stocks that survive this screen that make it onto one of the model portfolios in the MPT Review. Navellier offers conservative, moderately aggressive, and aggressive model portfolios for investors with $10,000, $75,000, $300,000, $500,000 or $1 million to invest.

If you are going to try to pick small company growth stocks on your own, you should be looking for most of the things described so far in this chapter. Look for those companies with a new product, service, or market niche. You also can use some of Navellier's screens on your own.

Foremost to consider is earnings growth, both historical and projected. You are looking for rapid historical growth, the higher the better. You can obtain earnings projections from Value Line or from your broker. Most analysts project earnings growth about two years into the future. You'll want to make sure growth is increasing at least as fast as it has historically.

Another area to consider is profit margin expansion. This is important because it shows that a company's operating efficiency is improving, and it is able to charge premium prices for its products, compared to companies with lower profit margins. Look for profit margins of 5% or more.

Looking for a record of positive earnings surprises by analysts may seem unusual, but it is very important when investing in small companies. Investors reward rapid earnings growth and love positive surprises. On the other hand, if a company checks in with earnings of even 1 cent below expectations, investors will often brutalize the stock price by selling their shares. There have been instances where a company lost 50% or more of its value in one day, because it's earnings did not meet analyst expectations.

**Small
Company
Funds**
If you choose to leave the stock selection in small company stocks to the experts, you should have no trouble finding a small company stock mutual fund. You should use the same selection criteria here as with large company funds: outstanding 10 year track record, consistency of management, and reasonable fees.

There are a couple of things that small company fund investors must pay attention to, in addition to the above characteristics. First, be wary of the way funds are classified. Some publications may list small company funds under different headings: aggressive growth or capital appreciation, for example. Because there is no uniform standard for naming funds, you may have to consult a prospectus to make sure you are investing in a small company fund.

One last thing to remember is that large size is not an advantage with small company funds. Because mutual funds are only permitted to hold up to 10% of any one company's outstanding shares, it becomes very hard for a large fund to keep investing in small companies. What will invariably happen is that they will have to begin creeping into mid-cap companies as they run out of investment candidates in small companies. Most good small company funds close to new investors after they reach a certain size and sometimes reopen after down periods in the market when people tend to panic and liquidate their shares.

Of course this is not a problem with the closed-end fund small company mutual fund investor. They are brought to market at the size the manager feels is best, to take advantage of a particular small company stock selection style. While there are not a whole lot of closed-end funds that invest in small company funds, you may get the opportunity to buy those available at a discount to net asset value.

The Bottom Line:

- If you are going to attempt to pick individual small company stocks, stick to a disciplined system or follow the advice of a small company professional.
- If you would like to stick with mutual funds, identify a true small company fund with a solid 10 year track record and consistency of management.
- You can also purchase unit investment trusts who invest in smaller companies.
- Compare the performance of the small company portfolio to the NASDAQ Composite index.
- Most conservative investors should have no more than 33%, and no less than 20%, of their equity money in small company stocks.

Footnotes

1   Ibbotson Associates, Stocks, Bonds, Bills and Inflation Yearbook, by Roger G. Ibbotson and Rex A. Sinquefield, 1995

2   Lee Kopp, Kopp Investment Advisors, 1995 Client Reception audio tape, 6600 France Avenue South, Suite 672, Edina, MN 55435, (612) 920-3322

3   Lee Kopp, Kopp Investment Advisors

4   How to Make Money In Stocks: A Winning System in Good Times or Bad, by William J. O'Neil, McGraw-Hill, 1991, page 23

5   Louis Navellier's MPT Review, P.O. Box 10012, Incline Village, NV, 89450, (800) 454-1395

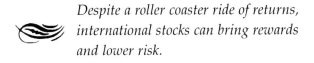

Despite a roller coaster ride of returns,
international stocks can bring rewards
and lower risk.

Chapter Fifteen
International Portfolio

Historically, American investors have found ample investment opportunities right in their own back yard. However, since world markets have been constantly changing and growing, the growth in investment options outside the U.S. has been dramatic.

As late as 1970, 70% of the world's stock market capitalization was based in the U.S. and 30% overseas. Now, 25 years later, almost the opposite is true. Sixty-seven percent of the investment opportunities on earth are found outside the U.S. The U.S. economy has reached a state of maturity, and there are now limits to its potential for rapid growth[1]. It may be possible to see the U.S. market capitalization number decrease even further in the years ahead.

While the idea of investing in foreign markets may seem appealing, it must be done with much caution. Foreign markets, unlike the U.S. market, are at varying levels of development. For example, in Europe, the securities markets are similar to those of the U.S., with stocks of well-known companies trading on liquid exchanges.

However, the fall of communism in Eastern Europe has opened new markets and opportunities, and has led to a growing demand for basic goods and services. These markets will be looking to Western Europe as producers of consumer goods. At the same time, investment opportunities continue in the developed markets of Western Europe as the trend of privatization of many publicly owned companies increases. Privatization refers to the sale of state-owned enterprises, like telephone companies, to the public. Privatization generally improves profitability and results in increased stock prices.

In the Pacific Basin, rapid growth is occurring in markets like Hong Kong, Korea, Singapore, Taiwan and Malaysia. Lower wages have led to rapid industrialization and economic expansion, with an expanding middle class and tremendous need for infrastructure development. Infrastructure is something that Americans take for granted each and every day. It is the basic transportation, communications, and utilities systems that a country has in place. Building and maintaining these systems is the first step in an emerging country's economic development and often provides for investment opportunities. It takes a great deal of capital to build these systems, and the companies involved tend to make money during the process.

Mexico, Argentina, Brazil, Chile, and Venezuela are some of the countries that make up the Latin American market. The move toward political and economic reform has lifted trade barriers and fueled large scale inflows of foreign capital into those countries. Investors are capitalizing on the same need for infrastructure that the Pacific Rim countries face[2].

The rapid economic growth of foreign countries can produce eye-popping stock market growth. The Austrian market was up 177% in 1985. The Mexican market was up 145% in 1991. The Turkish market was up an amazing 220% in 1993[3]. With returns like these, why don't we just scrap our U.S. investments and put all our money in the foreign markets? Quite simply because you can't have reward without risk. In late 1994 into 1995, the Mexico Fund, a closed end fund invested in Mexican equities, lost 65% of its value in just over 3 months.

Roller coaster returns notwithstanding, it's hard to ignore the longer-term results posted by the various foreign markets over the last ten years, ending 1993. Hong Kong annualized 36% over those ten years. Belgium's market returned 25.3%, Spain's 24.8%, and Austria's 23.5%. Far down the list, in 13th place, the U.S. markets returned 14.8% over the same period[4]. As a matter of fact, the U.S. stock market has ranked among the top five markets only three times during the 25 years ending 1993 — and not once as the top market![5]

A final argument for investing in foreign markets is that it may actually decrease portfolio volatility. The correlation between the performance of the U.S. market and that of foreign markets is often quite low. Correlation is a statistical measure of the degree to which prices in different markets move in tandem. Because each individual market tends to reflect its own set of monetary, fiscal and exchange rate policies, the price movement of various equity markets can often be in different directions. This action in price movement will produce an overall smoothing effect for the return of the whole equity portfolio.

Clearly, most investors should have some of their equity money in the foreign markets. The question is: how much? According to Morgan Stanley Capital International, an equity portfolio comprised of between 20% and 35% of non-U.S. stocks can add to return and actually lower overall risk[6].

Once you know how much to invest in the foreign markets, all that is left is to buy the securities. Unfortunately, this step is often more easily said than done. Buying individual stocks in the foreign markets is a very difficult undertaking, one which I do not recommend. Currency fluctuations, relatively low liquidity in some foreign markets, and the potential for political unrest are some of the major reasons why the average investor should steer clear of individual stocks. Another reason is that it is very difficult to get accurate financial information on a prospective company. Many foreign companies use different standards of accounting and financial disclosure than we do. The result is trying to compare apples to oranges, and you will often end up with lemons.

My investment of choice for the international markets is the closed-end mutual fund. There are many advantages of investing internationally in closed-end funds. The most important is that you get professional investment management. The managers of these funds often have offices in many of the countries in which they invest. That way, they have their "finger on the pulse" of the economy and immediate knowledge of other developments that can affect stocks in that market. They are also familiar with the currency and methods of accounting used in the country or countries where they are invested.

International closed-end stock funds also offer diversification between many different companies. Because of the potential volatility of these markets, holding hundreds of different companies can decrease the risk. Closed-end funds can also offer diversification between countries. Although there are many closed-end funds that invest solely in the securities of one country, several exist that invest in a whole region or in a composite of many "emerging market" countries.

For example, currently there are single country funds such as the Mexico Fund, the Brazil Fund, the India Fund, the Germany Fund, and the Portugal Fund. There are also regional funds like the Latin American Discovery Fund that invests in the countries of Latin America.

An example of a composite fund would be the GT Global Developing Markets Fund. This fund invests substantially all of its assets in the developing markets of Asia, Europe and Latin America. At the end of November 1995, the top countries in the portfolio were Brazil, Mexico, Argentina, Hong Kong, South Africa, South Korea, Poland, Bulgaria, United States, and Columbia[7].

How do you determine what countries or areas of the world are suitable for investment? That's a tough question if you are trying to pinpoint a specific country in which to invest. There are so many variables that it is impossible to be truly familiar with all of them unless you live in the prospective country, or at the very least keep up on news from the country regularly in an international newspaper or periodical.

For the most part, diversification over many countries is the best way to invest internationally. I recommend that average investors place the majority of their international money in composite regional or emerging market funds. At the time of publication, my international portfolio is made up of five funds, four regional and composite, and one single country fund. Single country funds are a much more targeted bet and are, therefore, much riskier.

It is helpful to watch the relationship between the price and the net asset value of international closed end funds. If the current discount is near the historical high, it may be a good time to invest in that fund. It usually means that most investors would rather be investing their money in some other country or region. That's often a good time to step in and buy shares in the fund.

Other Ways to Buy International Investments   Again, you should be sure your retirement plan portfolio is fully invested before you attempt to start any other savings. And, be sure that a proportionate amount of your retirement plan assets are invested in international stocks. Many 401(k) plans have begun to offer an international stock investment option. Those that don't, yet, probably will do so at some point in the future. As you have seen in the last 5 chapters, you may actually be able to nearly recreate the asset allocation strategies that I have presented in this book in your retirement plan. Other than the value stock strategy, more and more plans are offering enough options to diversify between the income, small and large company growth, and international asset classes.

The rapid growth in the open end mutual fund market has certainly not skipped over the international sector. Over the past several years, hundreds of international funds have come to the market. Because most of these funds are relatively new, there won't be many that pass the 10 year performance record screen so you may have to go a little shorter. You should still be looking for a fund that has been guided by the same manager for several years. Also, because of the expenses associated with investing internationally, the fees on these funds are slightly higher.

One more thing to remember about international funds is that different publications may have more than one heading for these funds. Generally, "international" means that the fund invests in companies excluding the United States. On the other hand, global usually means that the fund can invest part of its portfolio in shares of U.S. companies. Just to be safe, you should consult the prospectus to make sure of the fund's investment objectives. Some global funds have the ability to invest over 50% of assets in the United States.

When you intend to buy international positions, make sure that's what you get.

Finally, if you feel compelled to buy shares of stock in international companies, I would recommend that you buy American Depository Receipts (ADRs). An ADR is a receipt for the shares of a foreign-based company held by a U.S. bank. Instead of buying shares of the company in the overseas market on which it trades, Americans can buy shares in the form of ADRs. Shareholders are entitled to all dividends and capital gains resulting from the purchase and sale of these shares. Additionally, a company with a listed ADR is required to supply investors with annual and interim reports as they would with any U.S. investment. Some ADR issuers may choose to distribute other corporate information as well.

The Bottom Line:

- Don't buy individual foreign stocks.
- If you want to attempt investing internationally, use mostly composite closed-end funds that invest in many countries or regions.
- If you are more comfortable with open-end funds, make sure you select a true international fund with a solid 10 year record and consistency of management.
- If you prefer holding individual stocks, consider American Depository Receipts (ADRs).
- Most conservative investors should have no more than 35%, and no less than 20%, of their equity money in international stocks.

Footnotes

1   Newgate Management Associates, 1995 Broadway, 12th floor, NY, NY 10023, brochure, 1994, page 6

2   The CountryFund Opportunity Trust brochure, 1994 series, Smith Barney, page 1

3   A Guide to International Investing, brochure, Smith Barney research, 1994

4   The CountryFund Opportunity Trust brochure, 1994 series, Smith Barney, page 2

5   A Guide to International Investing, brochure, Smith Barney research, 1994, page 1

6   Newgate Management Associates, 1995 Broadway, 12th floor, NY, NY 10023, brochure, (actual source: Morgan Stanley Capital International), 1994

7   G.T. Capital Management, Inc., Fact Sheet, November 21, 1995

PART THREE

Putting It All Together

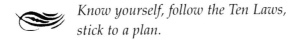

Know yourself, follow the Ten Laws, stick to a plan.

Putting It All Together

Now that you have finished reading all of the laws, theories, concepts, and strategies presented in this book, you are ready to move on to the next step: putting it all together and making it happen for yourself.

The checklist below is designed to help you review some of the concepts presented in this book. Each item on the list is important to your financial future. When you have already completed the exercises presented in the previous chapters, you may have learned a few things that may change your previous answers. These questions have been designed to highlight those areas that may have changed after reading the whole book.

Wealth In a Decade Plan and Checklist

_____I believe it is possible for me to become wealthy in ten years.

_____I have defined wealth for myself. This is what it means to me:_____

_____

_____

_____I have financial goals and have identified ways to reach them. My goals are: _____

_____

_____

_____

_____

   This is how I will reach those goals: _____

_____

_____

_____

   This is the timeline I have set for myself in reaching my goals: _____

_____

_____

_____

_____

____I have identified mentors who will help me reach my goals. My mentors are: _____

_____

_____

_____I know wealth is not based on what I make, but on what I spend. Here are some ways I have decided to cut expenses:_____

_____

_____

_____

_____I have identified ways to save 15% per year. I will use the following steps to increase my savings to 35%:_____

_____

_____

_____I have insulated myself from unexpected and expected financial drains with a rainy day fund and proper insurance. I do not include my rainy day fund in my portfolio or include it in my asset allocation decisions.

_____I know that my portfolio must change as circumstances change. Some changing circumstances for me will be: _____

_____

_____

_____ I will use investing disciplines whenever possible so my emotions will not manage my money for me.

_____I understand the power of compound interest and have set a long time horizon. I will make sure that the investments I buy match my time horizon.

_____I have maximized my contributions to my retirement plan. If I don't have access to a company plan, I will utilize an IRA account.

_____I know which investments would amount to gambling with my money and I have avoided them.

_____My personal risk tolerance is: _____

_____I have planned for inflation and will fight it by investing a portion of my portfolio in stocks.

_____I know how to monitor my assets and I involve my spouse/partner in monitoring.

_____I know what indices to use to insure accurate monitoring. They are: _____

_____I know how to balance and rebalance my portfolio by buying low and selling high.

_____Here are the ways I have chosen to minimize my taxes and maximize my estate growth: _____

_____

_____

_____I have decided to do my investing for myself using mutual funds and individual stocks and bonds.

_____I have decided to seek the help of a financial advisor. I will still monitor the portfolio so I can hold him/her responsible.

_____ I need $_____ from my portfolio to live on. This means that at 8% I must devote $_____ to meeting this income requirement. For example: I need $200 a month to live on. $200 x 12 months = $2400/.08 = $30,000 of my portfolio must be devoted to meeting this income need.

_____ My age dictates that I have _____% (minimum 50%) or $_____ of my portfolio in income securities (including the amount necessary to support my income requirement) following the conservative strategy developed in the book. For example: Age 35, 50% in income securities. Age 50, 50% in income securities. Age 75, 75% in income securities.

_____ I know how to structure my income portfolio ladder. It will extend _____ years.

_____ My equity portfolio comprises _____% of my portfolio (100 - age, maximum 50%) following the conservative strategies developed in the book.

_____ My equity portfolio will be invested in the following asset classes:

Value Stocks	_____%	$_____
Large Company Growth Stocks	_____ %	$_____
Small Company Stocks	_____ %	$_____
International Stocks	_____ %	$_____
High Risk	_____ %	$_____

_____ Using the strategy developed in the book, my value portfolio will be made up of:_____

_____ I will use the Dow Jones Industrial Average to compare the performance of the value portfolio.

_____ using the concepts developed in the book, my large company growth portfolio will be made up of: _____

_____

_____

_____ I will use the S&P 500 index to compare the performance of the large company growth portfolio.

_____Using the concepts developed in the book, my small company portfolio will be made up of: _____

_____

_____

_____ I will use the NASDAQ Composite index to compare the performance of the small company portfolio.

_____ Using the concepts developed in the book, my international portfolio will be made up of: _____

_____

_____

_____ I will use the Morgan Stanley EAFE index to compare the performance of the international portfolio.

_____ I know where to get more information. I will utilize the following materials that Brett recommended: _____

_____

_____

If you have completed this check list, you have a good handle on your investments and are probably on your way to becoming wealthy.

"One Dollar"

One dollar at a time, a hundred pennies and ten thin dimes.
Some people lose is, some people save it
One dollar at a time.

There's no magic, there's no secret, there's no great big mystery
Time and discipline and great determination
That's the way it's got to be

One dollar at a time, one hundred pennies and ten thin dimes
Some people lose it, whoops!
Some people save it, uh, huh huh
One dollar at a time. Yeah! Yeah!

Two bits, four bits, six bits a dollar
Save your money, stand up and holler
It's one hundred pennies and ten thin dimes
Whoa now, some people are gonna lose it, don't you know
Some people are gonna save it
One dollar at a time.

Dollar after dollar, and time after time
Watch it keep on coming, a hundred pennies and ten thin dimes
That's the way it's gonna be
Some people lose it, some people save it
One dollar at a time.

Music and Lyrics by Ken Medema
written for *Wealth in a Decade*

"Wealth In A Decade"

Chorus

Wealth in a decade, this is the name of a dream
Wealth in a decade, it's not so crazy as it seems
You need no oil wells in your back yard
No lucky breaks, no great clandestine schemes
Wealth in a decade and you can live this dream

Ten short years and a plan you will stay with, is all you really need
You can build a better future for yourself, but you must take the lead
Ten short years and the heart and the will to do what you know you've
got to do
You can reap the rewards of a job well done but it all depends on you

Repeat Chorus

Music and Lyrics by Ken Medema
written for *Wealth in a Decade*

"Here and Now"

Well I've been waiting and I can't wait any longer
And I don't have the time for these detours anymore
I'm getting restless and the feeling's getting stronger
And I know I must go where I dared not go before

Now I see it stretching out like a throughway
And it leads me to places I've never, never been
Time to travel, travel down this new way
I am turning the corner and this is the way I begin

Chorus
Here and now I know that I can change my life
I can re-arrange my life and turn it right around
Here and now I'll take a new direction
'Cause I'm on my way headed for higher ground
Yes I'm on my way, now I am freedom bound

I see people caught between the falling rocks
Or maybe driving down a dead end street with no way through
Life gets dreary between the rock slides and the road blocks
Or when your driving round that round about
And you don't do what you know you've got to do

And now I see it stretching out like a highway
And it leads me over the wild and treacherous land
The road is calling and I think it's going my way
Got a map on the dash, and I'm taking the wheel in my hand

Repeat Chorus

Bridge
Watching out for the mountains and the valleys
Bright eyes peeled for the curves along the way
Stopping now and then to read the instructions again
It's a long, long road but it leads to a better day

Repeat Chorus

Music and Lyrics by Ken Medema
written for *Wealth in a Decade*

Appendix

There are many resources that can help you along the way, particularly if you are a novice investor or if you are going to manage all your investments yourself. These resources include other books, seminars, newsletters, and software programs that you can consult. Because one of my goals with this book was simplicity, I chose to omit a lot of the detail that might have bogged certain readers down, such as "what is a bond?" Obviously, by doing so, I may have left novice investors with some unanswered questions. Consulting these other materials should help you with most of your questions, or give you some new ideas if you are an experienced investor.

Books

The Beardstown Ladies' Common Sense Investment Guide, by Beardstown Ladies Investment Club, with Leslie Whitaker, Hyperion, 1994. 272 pages. $19.95

Description: The "Ladies" here are 16 women, average age 55, of an Illinois river town whose investment club, since 1984, has scored an average 23.4% annual return - twice the rate of the bellwether S&P 500 index. The book is chock-full of family-finance anecdotes, firsthand reports on regional industry, case histories of stocks bought and sold, recommended research tools and the actual minutes (with portfolio changes) of meetings during the banner year of 1991.

The Personal Investor's Complete Book of Bonds, by Donald R. Nichols, Longman Financial Services Pub.: (Distributed by Longman Trade), 1989. 256 pages. $19.95

Description: Nichols, author of several other investment books, provides a complete, up-to-date discussion of the various types of bonds and assesses risks and potential yields. He suggests how to use bonds in planning and saving for special situations such as college tuition or retirement.

How to Live Within Your Means and Still Finance Your Dreams, by Robert A. Ortalda, Jr., CPA, Simon and Schuster, 1990. 352 pages.

The Great Boom Ahead: Your comprehensive guide to personal and business profit in the new era of prosperity, by Harry S. Dent, Jr., Hyperion, 1993. 273 pages. $10.95

Description: Business consultant Dent contends that economic trends are highly predictable and forecasts an unprecedented boom over the next decade.

Technotrends: How to use technology to go beyond your competition, by Daniel Burrus with Roger Gittines, Harper Business, 1993. 376 pages. $25

Description: The author discusses technological innovations such as electronic notepads, neural networks, diamond thin-films, etc. He aims to demonstrate how best to utilize these new tools to gain advantage in business, government, education, and everyday life.

Unlimited Power: The new science of personal achievement, by Anthony Robbins, Simon and Schuster, 1986. 361 pages. $16.95

Description: This is a comprehensive and intelligent success achievement program for setting and following through with personal and professional goals by the California behaviorist

who popularized the method of "neurolinguistic program-
ming" (NLP), or control of mind over body. One of the best
books on goal setting, behaviour modification and understanding the power of beliefs.

*60 Minute Estate Planner: Fast and easy illustrated plans to save
taxes, avoid probate, and maximize inheritance,* by Sandy F.
Kraemer, Prentice Hall, 1994. 256 pages. $29.95

Description: The Sixty-Minute part of Kraemer's title refers
to the time one will need to spend with a lawyer, accountant,
trust officer, or financial planner after taking the time to prepare oneself using the advice and information Kraemer presents in this understandable, helpfully illustrated guide to
saving taxes, avoiding probate, and maximizing inheritance.

Seminars

The Silva Method - Many think that geniuses are born, Jose
Silva believes they are made. Teaches the skills and strate-
gies of genius, including goal setting and comprehension.
Silva International, 210-722-6391

Financial Mastery - Tony Robbins assembles a number of
highly regarded people as faculty members and conducts a
very comprehensive seminar in places like Hawaii, Aspen,
and Phoenix. Teaches you how to earn more, protect what
you have, make your money grow, leverage your wealth, and
how to enjoy the whole process. The seminar also provides
numerous opportunities for mentoring.
Robbings Research International, 800-445-8183

Computer Programs

Quicken; published by Intuit; $19.99 in Windows; new version will be out in late October for $39.99; to order from publisher: (800) 624-8742.

Description: Personal financial management software system.

Newsletters/Market Letters

MPT Review, by Louis Navellier; (800) 454-1395; monthly newsletter; $225 per year, $49 for 2 months

Description: Quantitative analysis of primarily small and mid-size publicly traded companies.

Closed End Fund Digest, by Madent Publishing, Inc.: 800-282-2335

Description: Newsletter

The Hulbert Financial Digest, by Mark Hulbert; (703) 683-5905; E-mail address "HFD@DELPHI.COM"; $37.50 five-issue trial subscription; $135 per year.

Description: Newsletter which rates the performance of other investment advisory services.

The H.S. Dent Forecast: The Economic Guide for Effective Financial Decision Making, by Harry Dent. (415) 572-2879 Fax (415) 312-9516; bi-monthly newsletter; $148 per year (6 issues)

Description: A bi-monthly newsletter designed to keep investors and business people informed of the key trends and developments in the economy that will affect their most strategic investment decisions.

R=

N	4%	5%	6%	7%	8%	9%	10%	11%	12%	13%	14%	15%	20%	25%	30%
1	1	1	1	1	1	1	1	1	1	1	1	1	1	1	1
2	2.04	2.05	2.06	2.07	2.08	2.09	2.10	2.11	2.12	2.13	2.14	2.15	2.20	2.25	2.30
3	3.12	3.15	3.18	3.21	3.24	3.27	3.31	3.34	3.37	3.40	3.44	3.47	3.64	3.81	3.99
4	4.24	4.31	4.37	4.44	4.50	4.57	4.64	4.71	4.77	4.85	4.92	4.99	5.36	5.76	6.18
5	5.41	5.52	5.63	5.75	5.86	5.98	6.10	6.22	6.35	6.48	6.61	6.74	7.44	8.20	9.04
6	6.63	6.80	6.97	7.15	7.33	7.52	7.71	7.91	8.11	8.32	8.53	8.75	9.93	11.25	12.75
7	7.89	8.14	8.39	8.65	8.92	9.2	9.48	9.78	10.08	10.40	10.73	11.06	12.91	15.07	17.58
8	9.21	9.54	9.89	10.26	10.63	11.02	11.43	11.85	12.3	12.75	13.23	13.72	16.49	19.84	23.85
9	10.58	11.02	11.49	11.97	12.48	13.02	13.57	14.16	14.77	15.41	16.08	16.78	20.79	25.80	32.01
10	12.00	12.57	13.18	13.81	14.48	15.19	15.93	16.72	17.54	18.42	19.33	20.30	25.95	33.25	42.61
11	13.48	14.20	14.97	15.78	46.64	17.56	18.53	19.56	20.65	21.81	25.04	24.34	32.15	42.56	56.40
12	15.02	15.91	16.87	17.88	18.97	20.14	21.38	22.71	24.13	25.65	27.27	29.00	39.58	54.20	74.32
13	16.62	17.71	18.88	20.14	21.49	55.95	24.52	26.21	28.02	29.98	32.08	34.35	48.49	68.76	97.62
14	18.29	19.59	21.01	22.55	24.21	26.01	27.97	30.09	32.39	34.88	37.58	40.50	59.19	86.94	127.91
15	20.02	21.57	23.27	25.12	27.15	29.36	31.77	34.40	37.28	40.41	43.84	47.58	72.03	109.68	167.28
16	21.82	23.65	25.67	27.88	30.32	33.00	35.95	39.19	42.75	46.67	50.98	55.71	87.44	138.10	218.47
17	23.69	25.84	28.21	30.84	33.75	36.97	40.54	44.50	48.88	53.73	59.11	65.07	105.93	173.63	285.01
18	25.64	28.13	30.90	33.99	37.45	41.30	45.59	50.39	55.75	61.72	68.39	75.83	128.11	218.04	371.51
19	27.67	30.53	33.76	37.37	41.44	46.01	51.15	56.93	63.44	70.74	78.96	88.21	154.74	273.55	483.97
20	29.77	33.06	36.78	40.99	45.76	51.16	57.27	64.20	72.05	80.94	91.02	102.44	186.68	342.94	630.16
25	41.64	47.72	54.86	63.24	73.10	84.70	98.34	114.41	133.33	155.62	181.87	212.79	471.98	1054.70	2348.80
30	56.08	66.43	79.05	94.46	113.28	136.30	164.49	199.02	241.33	293.19	356.78	434.74	1181.80	3227.10	8729.90
35	73.65	90.32	111.43	138.23	172.31	215.71	271.02	341.29	431.66	546.68	693.57	881.71	2948.30	9856.70	32422.00
40	95.02	120.80	154.76	199.63	259.05	337.88	442.59	581.82	767.09	1013.70	1342.00	1779.00	7343.80	33088.00	120392.00
45	121.02	159.70	212.74	285.74	386.50	525.85	718.90	986.63	1358.20	1874.16	2590.50	3585.10	18281.00	91831.00	447019.00

Author Feedback

Dear Reader,

If you would like more information from me, there are many ways that I, too, can be of service. In addition to this book, I also offer an ten-cassette audio tape series based on the book, for those who like to listen rather than to read. There is also a software program, in a CD-ROM version, that is available to help guide you through the concepts presented in this book. The software uses outcome-based education techniques, and it will help you take all of this information and transfer it from an intellectual understanding to applied wisdom.

Also, I am constantly conducting live seminars throughout the country. These seminars go into much greater detail and focus on "hands on, personalized" learning. There are seminars available for both beginning investors and those who have already accumulated a portfolio. If you like what you see at my seminars, I am also available to speak to private audiences or organizations.

Finally, your experiences and opinions are important to me. I invite you to complete the form on the next page and mail it to me, or call 1-612-672-9497. My America Online email address is machtig1@aol.com.

My warmest regards,

Brett A. Machtig
Author, *Wealth in a Decade*

Hi Brett!

The most helpful thing in your book, *Wealth in a Decade,* was: _____

_____

_____

I still have questions about:_____

_____

_____

A situation I have found confusing is:_____

_____

_____

My personal success with investing is: _____

_____

_____

_____

My favorite investment products are: _____

_____

_____

Because: _____

_____

_____

_____

_____

Please mail this form to me: Brett Machtig, P. O. Box 50657, Minneapolis, Minnesota 55657.

Thank you so much for your feedback, and may every financial success be yours!

Also available:

The Great Boom Ahead Series by Harry S. Dent, Jr.

Harry Dent speaks on future trends bringing exciting new research from a depth of hands-on business experience. He applies basic principles of business strategy, finance, and marketing research to me economy and comes up with understandable and highly contrary forecasts. Although he forebodes mild setbacks between mid 1995 and 1996, he brings a uniquely positive view of the future into practical application at all levels: from business strategy, to jobs and changes in the workplace, to investment.

"Harry Dent's brilliant synthesis of society's shifting trends provides a much-needed antidote to today's overdose of gloom-and-doom economic forecasts. Use the insights in *The Great Boom Ahead* to find opportunities in what many will perceive as an uncertain world."- Anthony Robbins, author of *Unlimited Power* and *Awaken the Giant Within*

Investment Strategies for the Roaring 2000s
8 cassette tapes with self-study workbook. The most current and thorough explanation of Mr. Dent's breakthrough tools for future forecasting.   Normal price $198.00.

H.S. Dent Forecast
Bimonthly economic newsletter with frequent updates that keeps subscribers abreast of likely changes in the economy and financial markets and current with updates to Mr. Dent's research and long term forecasts.   Normal price $148.00.
Call for a free trial issue.

The Great Boom Ahead
Paperback version of Mr. Dent's most popular book on the future of our economy and the types of investments and companies that will prosper.
ISBN 1-56282-758-8 $10.95. Quantity discounts available.
Hyperion. Revised in 1995.

The Great Jobs Ahead
Paperback version of 1995 release on the trends that are reshaping our jobs and workplace.
ISBN: 0-312-11835-X $19.95. Quantity discounts available.
Hyperion.

Get An Edge On Tomorrow
From One of the World's Leading Technology Forecasters and Strategists...Daniel Burrus

Technotrends: How To Use Technology To Go Beyond Your Competition

Do you need to gain a major competitive advantage? Do you need to create a winning strategic plan? Learn by example to apply the "new technological tools" and the "new business rules" that are already transforming decision-making and management processes worldwide! This book provides breakthrough strategies necessary for anyone interested in creating a winning action plan!

"Absolutely fascinating! Breathes hope for all of us who are intimidated by change and technology." -Stephen R. Covey, author of *The 7 Habits of Highly Effective People*

"I have read the future and it is...*Technotrends!*...Visionary insights that translate immediately to the bottom line." -Harvey MacKay, author of *Swim With The Sharks Without Being Eaten Alive*

Hardcover   Item #407   List $25.00   Special $20.00 each
Paperback   Item #407P   List $14.00   Special $11.20 each

The Technotrends Business Strategy Game

Join the many corporations and organizations developing winning strategies by using the same deck of cards as described in the book *Technotrends*. Determine innovative future directions by using the 24 "New Tool" cards and the 30 "New Rule" cards in a problem-solving game of "Business Solitaire." Or play with colleagues and business partners to define new ways to go beyond your competition using the new tools and business rules of the future.

"Playing the card game is like hiring a consultant or attending a two-day seminar. It pushes you toward new ways of looking at your company, its customers, and your competition. The card game is a way to become aware of the driving forces - tools and rules - that will revitalize American business as we enter the 21st century." -Successful Meetings

Item #701   List $12.95   Special $10.95

How to Live Within Your Means and Still Finance Your Dreams
by Robert A. Ortalda, Jr., CPA

If the financial institutions in your "portfolio" all have names like Visa, MasterCard and American Express...

If you need help focusing on the future instead of spending in the present...

If you feel that you're better at spending then you'll ever be at saving...

If you and your spouse don't agree about handling your money...

If you really want to get your arms around your personal budget...

...then I strongly recommend Bob Ortala's *How to Live Within Your Means and Still Finance Your Dreams.*

Bob's observations on the economics of the baby boom generation have won him significant media attention. But more importantly, he provides down-to-earth advice for solving the problems and taking advantage of the opportunities facing this vast group of young adults.

Bob has spoken on personal finance to audiences around the country and made hundreds of media appearances. His system and his delivery are acclaimed by laymen and financial professionals alike as sophisticated, workable, wryly humours and uniquely understanding of the baby boomer's predicament.

Bob's revolutionary book makes budgeting not only possible—but rewarding. He presents a unique, realistic, step-by-step system for getting the things you want, when you want them—without spending yourself into debt.

This book is a must if you want to take control of your personal finances, reduce your dependence on credit, and still achieve your personal dreams.

ISBN 0-671-69607-6 (Fireside) $11.00 Paperback

Order Form

Fax order to 612-559-5696 or mail to IGI, 14550 28th Ave. North, Mpls, MN 55447
To order by phone, call Brett at 800-334-1515.

item	qty	price	total
Wealth in a Decade: A Fresh Approach to Financial Freedom, Security, and Control — Hard Cover Edition		$24.95	
Wealth in a Decade: A Fresh Approach to Financial Freedom, Security, and Control — Complete Ten Audio Cassette Series		$129.95	
Wealth in a Decade Series: Get Smart, Get Out of Debt and On the Road to Finacial Success — Two Audio Cassettes and Workbook		$39.95	
Wealth in a Decade Series: Life is Short – Live it Wealthy: How to Go from Zero to Wealthy in Ten Years — Six Audio Cassettes and Workbook		$79.95	
Wealth in a Decade Series: How to Shape up Your Portfolio and Get the Most from Your Investments — Four Audio Cassettes and Workbook		$69.95	
Wealth in a Decade Series: The Introduction to Wealth in a Decade and Author Brett A. Machtig — One 90-minute Audio Cassette and Brochure		$7.00	
Wealth in a Decade Series: The Introduction to Wealth in a Decade and Author Brett A. Machtig — 10–minute Keynote Video and Brochure		$10.00	
Wealth in a Decade: A Fresh Approach to Financial Freedom, Security, and Control — IBM Computer Slide Show		$150.00	
Wealth in a Decade: A Fresh Approach to Financial Freedom, Security, and Control — Keynote Speaking or Workshops		Call for Quote	
Technotrends: How to Use Technology to Go Beyond Your Competition by Daniel Burrus		$14.00	
The Great Boom Ahead by Harry S. Dent, Jr.		$10.95	
How to Live Within Your Means and Still Finance Your Dreams by Bob Ortalda, CPA		$11.00	
Subtotal			
add $5.00 shipping and handling			
Sales Tax (MN residents add 6.5%, downtown Mpls add 7%)			
TOTAL			

Name_____ Street Address_____

City, State, Zip_____ Phone (required)_____
❑ Check/Money Order enclosed for $_____
Make payable to Image Publishing Group. No cash or C.O.D.'s please.

❑ Visa   ❑ MasterCard

Account #_____Exp. Date_____
Print name as it appears on card_____
Signature_____

Glossary of Common Investment Terms

ASSET ALLOCATION - How a portfolio is divided among different types of investments, usually stocks, bonds and cash. The goal of asset allocation is achieving the highest return possible without taking on more risk than the investor is comfortable with.

BALANCED PORTFOLIO - A portfolio containing roughly equal amounts in stocks and bonds.

BEAR MARKET - A period during which stock prices are declining.

BETA - A measure of a stock's movement relative to the market. If a stock moves more than the market, it carries a beta greater than on — less than the market, its beta is less than one.

BOND - A debt security representing a contractual agreement by a company or government to repay a borrowed money by a specified time at a specified rate.

BULL MARKET - A period during which stock prices are rising.

CAPITAL APPRECIATION - Increase in the price of an investment.

CAPITAL GAIN/LOSS - The profit (loss) that results from a change in the price of an asset. A realized gain (loss) occurs when an investment security is sold at a price above (below) its cost.

CAPITAL MARKET - A broad term encompassing all the securities markets in which stocks, bonds and money market instruments are traded.

CAPITAL PRESERVATION - An investment objective in which protecting the investor's initial investment from loss is the primary goal. A conservative investment objective.

CASH EQUIVALENT - Investments in short-term debt obligations issued by governments, banks and corporations that mature less than one year from issuance.

CLOSED-END MUTUAL FUND - A mutual fund that offers a fixed number of shares for sale and trades on a stock exchange.

COMMERCIAL PAPER - Unsecured debt generally issued by companies to meet short-term financing needs. Commercial paper represents a large portion of the money market.

COMMON STOCK - Security representing ownership interest in a company.

CONSUMER PRICE INDEX (CPI) - A common measure of inflation. The CPI is equal to the sum of prices of a number of goods purchased by consumers and weighted by the proportion each represents in a typical consumer's budget.

CONTRARIAN - An investor who purposely does to opposite of what most investors are doing. A contrarian investor tries to select securities that are out of favor with the market.

CREDIT QUALITY - A measure of the likelihood that a company will be able to make interest and principal payments on its bonds or other debt securities. Standard and Poor's Corporation and Moody's Investor Service rate the credit quality of publicly traded debt securities.

DIVERSIFICATION - The process of investing in a number of different types of investment classes to reduce the risk of poor performance by any one type of investment having a big impact on overall portfolio results.

DIVIDEND - Cash payment made by a company to stockholders.

DIVIDEND YIELD - Total amount of cash dividend received annually on a share of stock divided by the price of the stock.

EAFE INDEX - An abbreviation for the Morgan Stanley Capital International Europe, Australia and Far East index, an index of overseas stock performance.

EPS - Earnings per share; a company's net income divided by the total number of outstanding shares. Generally regarded as a measure of a firm's profitability.

EQUITY - The ownership interest of common and preferred stockholders in a company.

EXPECTED RETURN - The return investors anticipate they will receive on an investment over some future period. THe expected return is often unrealistically higher than the investors' actual realized return.

FINANCIAL GOALS - What investors would like to achieve with their investments, such as saving for retirement, funding educational expenses, paying for a major purchase in the future, etc.

FIXED INCOME INVESTMENTS - Debt securities, such as bonds and money market instruments, with specified interest and principal payment dates and amounts. Can also include preferred stock. Also known as simply income investments.

GROWTH STOCKS - Stocks of companies whose earnings are expected to grow rapidly.

INVESTMENT OBJECTIVE - The investment strategy followed by an individual investor or portfolio manager. Objectives could be designed to generate income, capital appreciation or a blend of both.

LIQUIDITY - The ease with which investments can be bought or sold quickly without having a major impact on the price of those investments.

MARKET CAPITALIZATION - The market value of a company. It equals the current stock price multiplied by the total number of shares outstanding.

MARKET CYCLE - Generally regarded as a period of 5 to 10 years.

MARKET TIMING - Attempting to sell investments before they decrease in value and buy when they are about to increase in value.

MONEY MARKET - The market in which short-term, highly liquid, low-risk assets such as Treasury bills, bank certificates of deposits (CDs), corporate commercial paper and banker's acceptances are traded.

MUTUAL FUND - An investment company that pools the money of many individuals and invests it on their behalf in accordance with predetermined investment objectives. There are two types of mutual funds — open and closed-end.

NOMINAL RETURN - The return of an investment , not adjusted for the effect of inflation.

OPEN-END MUTUAL FUND - A mutual fund that stands ready to issue and redeem shares of the fund as supply and demand dictate.

P/E RATIO - Stock price divided by the earnings per share (EPS). It represents the amount stock investors are willing to pay for $1 of the company's earnings. It is the most often quoted measure of stock valuation.

PERFORMANCE - The change in the value of a portfolio over a specific period of time. The overall performance of an investment includes both income and capital gains or losses.

PORTFOLIO - The combined securities held by an investor, no matter where they are held.

PORTFOLIO MANAGER - The individual or firm responsible for the day-to-day decisions involving an investment portfolio. The manager decides which stocks or bonds to buy or sell and when.

PRINCIPAL - The original amount invested in a security or portfolio.

REAL ESTATE INVESTMENT TRUST (REIT) - A company that manages a portfolio of real estate properties.

REAL RETURN - The return on an investment minus the effects of inflation.

RISK - The possibility that the actual return on an investment will be different from the expected return. In general, the greater the risk, the greater the possible return on an investment.

RISK-FREE INVESTMENT - A riskless investment; although there is really no such thing as a riskless investment, U.S. Treasury securities are considered risk-free investments.

S & P 500 - Market value index of stock market activity. Measures the performance of 500 widely held common stocks and is often used as a proxy for the stock market.

SECURITIES AND EXCHANGE COMMISSION (SEC) - A federal government agency, which was created by the Securities and Exchange Act of 1934, that regulates the securities industry and administers federal securities laws.

STOCKS - See COMMON STOCKS and EQUITY.

TIME HORIZON - The amount of time investors allow to achieve the expected return on their investments. Generally, the longer the time horizon, the more risk the investor can accept.

TOTAL RETURN - The total amount a given investment returns to investors, including any capital gains or losses and stock dividends or interest from interest bearing securities.

UNIT INVESTMENT TRUST (UIT) - A professionally selected, then essentially unmanaged portfolio of securities.

VALUE STOCKS - Stocks that are traded at a cheap price relative to the company's perceived worth.

VOLATILITY - The degree to which a portfolio's value moves up and down over time.

WEALTH - The state or condition of being able to live off of the income generated by one's investment portfolio.

Table of Illustrations

More praise for *Wealth in a Decade:*

Everyone should read this very timely book. We are going to see the greatest boom in history occur in the next decade as the huge baby boom generation moves into its peak spending years. Machtig presents a comprehensive, conservative approach to saving and building wealth in just a decade... and that is how long most of us have to get serious about securing our future before economic tides could turn against us.

> - Harry S. Dent, Jr., *The Great Boom Ahead, Job Shock*

Wealth in a Decade is an easy to follow roadmap to financial freedom. Anyone can benefit from Brett's practical approach and insight, no matter what their income or financial status. It will work, just do it!

> David L. Allen, Vice President/Branch Manager
> Prudential Securities, Inc.

Wealth in a Decade has certainly challenged my well-established spending patterns. And it has done it without any intimidating and complicated language. What a book!

> - Ken Medema, Briar Patch Music

There are many pressures that can destroy a family. Finances need not be one of them. *Wealth in a Decade* provides a system for financial security that is simple to understand, embrace, and follow. Incorporating this book's principles will eliminate your financial burdens and help you to achieve personal wealth. You and your family deserve the benefits of Brett's research and guidance.

> - John Crudele, CSP,
> *Making Sense of Adolescence: How to Parent from the Heart*

Wealth in a Decade

Are you financially secure? Imagine what it would be like to live off the return from your investments for the rest of your life. This book can guide you to accomplish this task in just ten years!

For the last 10 years, the author has interviewed financially successful people and conducted research on just how they became successful. The result is the program to accumulate wealth presented in this book. Inside you will learn:

- the 10 laws to achieve wealth
- what constitutes a good financial plan
- that modeling your investment behavior after successful people will help you achieve success
- how to obtain and appropriately use mentors
- it's not how much you earn, but how much you save that will determine whether you can become wealthy
- that making smart long term investments outperforms complicated short term high risk investments
- practical suggestions on debt reduction
- savings tips
- spending hints
- what investments to consider
- how to set up your investment portfolio
- how to set up and manage both large and small company portfolios
- a fresh approach to financial freedom that tells not only how to build wealth, but reduce stress
- how to live off the income generated from your investment portfolio
- and much, much more!

A teacher with a modest salary or a company president with yearly bonuses can both travel the road of disciplined investing and in a decade both will be able to retire with the lifestyle they're accustomed to living. *Wealth in a Decade* gives the direct and easy-to-understand answer to the question of financial security.

Take a hold of your financial destiny. It is never too soon or too late to do so. Open the pages of this book and, indeed, achieve wealth in a decade!

About the Author

Brett Machtig is First Vice president and Senior Portfolio Manager of the Minneapolis office of a major Wall Street brokerage firm, and has consulted for over ten years with investors of all types. Hi conducts public seminars, and is a featured keynote speaker on financial topics throughout the country. He is also author of one of the premier investment and client management software programs being used in the financial industry today.

Machtig has recently embarked on the creation of a program of books and other teaching materials to teach basic life skills in the public school system, including money management, the lessons of financial success, mentoring, and goal setting, and is now establishing a foundation to carry on this work.

Machtig has degrees in Accounting, Economics, and Business Management from MacMurry College and has attended Duke University's prestigious Fuqua School of Business Management. He lives in Minneapolis with his wife, Mary, and young son Jonathan.

Wealth In A Decade